Hugging the Gorilla

by Ruediger Rey

Hugging the Gorilla

a little incomplete Sales Book

Dedicated to

Dad
one of the toughest negotiators I ever met
gone far too soon.

Mom,

my wife Petra,
my daughter Isabella and my son Dominik
who suffered all the way because of my workaholism,

my Mentors and friends, namely
Reiner H., Franz A.

and my apprenticeship supervisor
Hannes L.

Thank you.

Also thank you to those who always say
"you will not make it"

to the non believers in success
and those who try to make people small.

Cheers to you.
You were – and still are – wrong.

Foreword

Hugging the Gorilla: A Little Incomplete Sales Book

Sales is as much about courage as it is about strategy, and Hugging the Gorilla captures this duality perfectly. The "gorilla" represents the ultimate decision-makers — the influential individuals whose buy-in can make or break a deal. These are the high-stakes players who hold the power to shape outcomes, yet many salespeople shy away from engaging with them directly. It's easier to work around the edges, staying in familiar, low-risk territory.

But true success in sales demands boldness. It requires the courage to step out of your comfort zone, to face the fear of rejection, and to actively seek out and connect with those who matter most. "Hugging the gorilla" is about doing just that — embracing the challenge of building trust and having impactful conversations with key stakeholders who can truly move the needle.

At the same time, sales is never a finished game. That's why Hugging the Gorilla is also a little incomplete sales book. It doesn't claim to offer all the answers or a definitive formula for success. Instead, it serves as a flexible playbook — a resource of strategies, insights, and principles designed to be tailored to your unique challenges.

Sales evolves with every market trend, every new customer, and every unforeseen challenge.

No single book could claim to be "complete" because the learning never ends. This book acknowledges that reality, giving you tools to adapt and grow while encouraging you to approach every situation with creativity, courage, and resilience.

In these pages, you'll find guidance on how to prepare for critical conversations, engage meaningfully with top decision-makers, and build trust with those who have the power to shape outcomes. It's about facing the gorilla head-on and coming out stronger, more capable, and more confident.

At its core, Hugging the Gorilla: A Little Incomplete Sales Book is both a call to action and a companion for your sales journey. It's about the boldness to reach higher and the humility to keep learning, adapting, and refining your craft.

Yours,
Ruediger Rey

October 2024

CHAPTER 1: TODAY'S B2B MARKET HAS CHANGED DRAMATICALLY – BECOMING YOUR CUSTOMER'S TRUSTED ADVISOR IS KEY! 10

CHAPTER 2: IT'S NOT ABOUT HOW MANY CONTACTS YOU HAVE — IT'S ABOUT HAVING THE RIGHT ONES 18

CHAPTER 3: VISITING EXHIBITIONS AND CONFERENCES – ALWAYS GO WITH A PLAN 24

CHAPTER 4: WHY INBOUND LEADS ARE GOOD, BUT TARGETED OUTBOUND LEADS ARE BETTER 32

CHAPTER 5: WHY PIPELINE IS KEY AND WHY MANY SALES REPS CONFUSE THE FUNNEL WITH THE PIPELINE 40

CHAPTER 6: CREATE A PITCH THAT BRINGS VALUE TO YOUR CUSTOMERS – DON'T SELL FEATURES, SELL VALUE! 50

CHAPTER 7: GORILLAS DON'T BITE! – WHY IT'S IMPORTANT TO TALK TO THE PERSON WITH POWER 58

CHAPTER 8: SWEEP THE FLOOR BUT ALWAYS HAVE AN EYE ON THE CEILING – BALANCING SHOP FLOOR INSIGHTS AND DECISION-MAKER PRIORITIES 66

CHAPTER 9: UNDERSTANDING THE CUSTOMER – WHAT KEEPS THEM AWAKE AT NIGHT 74

CHAPTER 10: WHY BANT IS THE KEY: HOW TO ENSURE YOU HAVE BUDGET, AUTHORITY, NEED, AND TIMING (BANT) COVERED 84

CHAPTER 11: MAKE IT EASY FOR YOUR CUSTOMER TO BUY FROM YOU – NOBODY WANTS TO GET SOLD, EVERYONE WANTS TO BUY 92

CHAPTER 12: AS A SALESPERSON – BE ON TOP OF THE PROCESS 100

CHAPTER 13: CUSTOMER IS (NOT ALWAYS) KING — WHEN TO STEP BACK OR WALK AWAY 108

CHAPTER 14: MAKE THE DEAL HAPPEN – CLOSE WHEN THE DEAL IS CLOSABLE 116

CHAPTER 15: PITFALLS – THE ENDLESS TEST INSTALLATION 125

CHAPTER 16: FACED WITH AN RFQ YOU HAVEN'T INFLUENCED? WHAT YOU CAN DO TO WIN 133

CHAPTER 17: TALK ON EYE LEVEL: YOU ARE THE DOCTOR TO EASE YOUR CUSTOMER'S PAIN 141

CHAPTER 18: TOOLS MAKE YOUR LIFE EASIER 149

CHAPTER 18: YOU DON'T ALWAYS NEED TO TELL THE BAD THINGS IF YOU'RE NOT ASKED! 157

CHAPTER 19: FORGET BANT. FOR COMPLEX SALES SITUATIONS, MEDPICC IS A BETTER METHOD 165

SOURCES FOR "HUGGING THE GORILLA – OR MY LITTLE INCOMPLETE SALES BOOK" 175

WHY SHOULD YOU BUY "HUGGING THE GORILLA"? 182

Chapter 1: Today's B2B Market Has Changed Dramatically – Becoming Your Customer's Trusted Advisor Is Key!

The B2B sales game isn't what it used to be. Gone are the days when buyers depended on salespeople for product information, pricing, and recommendations. Thanks to the explosion of information available online, today's B2B buyers are smarter, more independent, and in full control of their own decision-making process.

These buyers have access to everything—product comparisons, reviews, case studies, and expert opinions—before they even consider speaking to a sales rep. By the time you enter the conversation, they've already done their homework. So, what's your role in this new landscape? You've got to become *more* than a salesperson. You've got to evolve into a *trusted advisor*.

In the modern B2B market, being a trusted advisor is no longer just a nice-to-have—it's essential. Your job isn't just to sell a product; it's to help your customer solve complex problems, guide them through strategic decisions, and offer insights they didn't even know they needed. This chapter explores the radical changes in today's B2B market and shows you how to adapt by becoming the advisor your customers can't do without.

How the B2B Market Has Change

Buyers Have More Information Than Ever

Today's B2B buyers come to the table *fully loaded*. Before they ever speak to you, they've researched your product, checked out your competitors, read customer reviews, and probably already have a sense of pricing. The playing field is leveled—buyers no longer rely on sales reps for basic information.

What they need from you is something they can't get from a Google search: *tailored, actionable insights* that go beyond the facts they already know.
Longer Buying Cycles with More Stakeholders

Buying decisions have become more complex. In many cases, you're not just dealing with one decision-maker — you've got a room full of stakeholders from finance, IT, operations, and maybe even legal. That means longer sales cycles, more negotiations, and different agendas to navigate.

Being a trusted advisor means you've got to speak the language of each stakeholder and understand their unique concerns. You're not just selling a product — you're guiding an entire organization through a decision-making process.

Buyers Are Less Receptive to Traditional Sales Tactics

The hard sell? Dead. Today's buyers can spot a pushy, self-serving sales pitch from a mile away, and nothing will make them disengage faster. Buyers want someone who takes a consultative approach, focusing on their problems, not the rep's quota.

As a trusted advisor, your mission is clear: help the buyer make the best decision for their business — even if that means recommending alternatives or pointing them in a direction that doesn't involve your product. The goal is long-term value, not a short-term sale.

The Rise of Customer Experience

In the new B2B world, *customer experience* reigns supreme. Price and features alone aren't enough anymore — buyers care about the overall experience they have with you, from the first conversation to post-sale support. A seamless, positive experience is often the difference between winning and losing a deal.

Being a trusted advisor means elevating the customer experience. You're there to provide value at every touchpoint, from insightful advice in the early stages to support after the contract is signed. You're not just closing deals — you're building partnerships.

What It Means to Be a Trusted Advisor

You're More Than a Salesperson – You're a Problem Solver
A trusted advisor doesn't just pitch products — they solve problems. You need to dig deep into your customer's pain points and understand their goals. When you truly understand what keeps your customer up at night, you can offer insights and solutions that go beyond just selling your product.

As a trusted advisor, you:

Listen carefully to understand your customer's real needs. Offer strategic advice, even if it means recommending solutions outside your product line. Position yourself as a partner in their success, not just a salesperson trying to hit a number.

Build Long-Term Relationships, Not Short-Term Transactions

The trusted advisor plays the long game. Your goal isn't just to close the deal and move on — it's to become an integral part of your customer's success story. That means understanding their business deeply, anticipating their future needs, and being there long after the ink dries on the contract.

When customers see you as a long-term partner, they're more likely to return, trust your advice, and recommend you to others.

Demonstrate Industry Knowledge and Expertise

It's not enough to know your product inside and out — you've got to understand the customer's industry, market challenges, and competitive landscape. The more you know, the more valuable you become.

When you can bring insights about industry trends, regulatory changes, or competitive threats, you're positioning yourself as someone with expertise that goes beyond the sale.

This kind of knowledge builds credibility and trust, which are the foundation of long-term relationships.

Be Transparent and Honest

Trust is earned through transparency. If your solution isn't the right fit, say so. If there's a challenge in meeting a deadline or staying within budget, be upfront. Customers value honesty, and they're far more likely to trust you in the long run if you're open about potential problems.

Being a trusted advisor means always putting your customer's best interests first, even when it's not convenient.

How to Become Your Customer's Trusted Advisor

Do Your Research

Being a trusted advisor starts with knowing your customer's business inside and out. That means doing your homework before every interaction. Understand their industry, their position in the market, and the challenges they face. When you're prepared with this level of knowledge, your conversations will be more meaningful, and your solutions will be more relevant.

Listen Before You Speak

Too many sales reps jump straight into their pitch. A trusted advisor listens first. Ask thoughtful questions, dig into your customer's challenges, and let them speak. The more you listen, the better you'll understand what they truly need—and the more accurately you can position your solution.

Offer Strategic, Tailored Insights

Once you've gathered information, it's time to provide *tailored*, strategic advice. Don't just rehash your product's benefits. Show your customer how it fits into their specific context and solves their unique problems. Position yourself as the go-to expert they can turn to when they need advice.

Follow Up and Stay Engaged

Your role as a trusted advisor doesn't end when the deal is signed. Keep in touch. Provide follow-up support, share relevant industry news, and stay connected. When your customer feels like you're invested in their long-term success, they'll keep coming back—and they'll send others your way.

Conclusion: Becoming a Trusted Advisor Is Key in Today's B2B Market

The B2B landscape has evolved, and so must your approach to sales. In today's world, buyers don't need a salesperson to tell them what they can already find online. They need a partner—a *trusted advisor*—who can help them navigate complexity, solve problems, and achieve their long-term goals.

If you want to thrive in this new environment, it's time to leave behind the old-school sales tactics and embrace the trusted advisor role. By building deeper relationships, offering strategic insights, and always putting your customer's needs first, you'll not only close more deals—you'll build a reputation that keeps customers coming back for more.

Your goal isn't just to sell. It's to become indispensable. That's the future of B2B sales.

Chapter 2: It's Not About How Many Contacts You Have — It's About Having the Right Ones

There's a seductive myth that success is tied to the length of your contact list. We've all met that salesperson, the one who proudly proclaims how many names they've stacked in their CRM like trophies, believing that every name represents potential wealth.

But here's the cold truth: You could have a list longer than the Great Wall, and if none of those people are the right ones, you've got nothing but dead leads.

Imagine throwing a party, inviting a thousand people, but not a single one is interested in what you're offering. That's not just awkward — that's a disaster.

The Key to Sales Success: Building the Right Network

Now, how do you avoid that disaster and fill your "party" with the right people—the ones who actually want what you're selling? Here's where the real magic happens. Successful salespeople don't chase after every shiny name like a kid collecting baseball cards. No, they operate with precision.

They focus on connecting with decision-makers, industry influencers, the movers and shakers who are genuinely aligned with their product or solution.

It's not about casting a wide net; it's about **casting a *smart* net**. And that's where we dive in: how to build a network that's not just full, but **full of the *right* people**. Whether you're leveraging the digital power of LinkedIn or shaking hands at an industry event, **it's all about strategy**.

LinkedIn: Your Digital Power Tool for Sales

Think of LinkedIn as the digital battlefield where the modern sales war is won. It's like walking into a networking event in your sharpest suit, but here's the kicker—you can't just stand there looking pretty. LinkedIn is only as powerful as you make it. If you want to make moves, you've got to work the system.

Here's how to dominate the platform like a pro:

1. **Targeted Outreach:** Let me be clear—random connection requests are like cold calls in the dark, and you know how effective those are. You don't just connect with anyone who has a pulse. Use LinkedIn's advanced search to find the decision-makers and influencers in your target market. And when you reach out, for the love of all things sales, *make it personal*. Reference a project they're working on, comment on a market trend, or hit them with a solution to a problem you know they're facing. Personalization is key; you're not a bot, so don't act like one.

2. **Active Engagement:** Adding someone to your list is just the first move. You've got to *stay* in the game. Like their posts, comment thoughtfully, share your insights—it's all about building a relationship. And relationships in sales are everything. If you want to be remembered, you've got to stay in front of them, consistently showing up and delivering value.

3. **Content Creation:** This is where you take the game to the next level. You want to be seen as the go-to expert in your field? Start putting out content that proves you're a leader. Write articles, share case studies, post market insights—whatever it takes to showcase your expertise. When your content is sharp and useful, the right people will come to *you*. It's not just about connecting, it's about attracting.

Industry Events: The Real Goldmine for Building Connections

While LinkedIn is a powerful digital tool, nothing beats the impact of face-to-face connections. There's a certain magic in shaking someone's hand, looking them in the eye, and building rapport. Industry events are where deals are born, but you can't just show up and wing it. You need a strategy.

1. **Research the Right Events:** Don't waste time attending every event that crosses your calendar. Be selective. Choose the ones that align with your target market and where decision-makers are likely to be present. You want to go where the action is, not just where the crowd gathers.

2. **Preparation is Power:** Showing up unprepared is the quickest way to blend into the background. Before you step foot into that event, know who's attending, what they care about, and how you can help them. When you approach someone with insight into their business, you're already setting yourself apart from the masses of generic salespeople.

3. **Follow Up Like a Pro:** You've met some key people, exchanged cards, and had good conversations. Now what? Here's where most people drop the ball—they *don't follow up*. That's like walking halfway through a deal and then leaving. Follow up fast, reference your conversation, and show that you're serious about solving their problem.

That's how you turn introductions into deals.

Conferences: The Olympics of Networking

If industry events are where deals are born, conferences are the Olympics of networking—high pressure, high reward. You're surrounded by industry heavyweights, and the opportunity is ripe for the taking. But you've got to come prepared to play at the highest level.

1. **Be Seen and Heard:** Don't sit in the audience and stay quiet. Ask smart questions during panels, offer your insights at roundtables, and be an active participant. The more visible you are, the more people will take notice of you. And when you bring value to the conversation, you're not just networking—you're branding yourself as an expert.

2. **Maximize the Informal Moments:** Some of the best connections happen in the downtime—during coffee breaks, lunches, or the after-event social. These informal moments are gold for building deeper, more personal relationships. Don't overlook them.

3. **Have Your Pitch Ready:** You never know when opportunity will strike, so always be ready with your elevator pitch. Keep it sharp, concise, and memorable. You might only have 30 seconds to impress someone, so make it count.

Conclusion: Quality Over Quantity

When it's all said and done, the size of your contact list doesn't matter. What matters is *who* is on that list. You don't need a sea of names—you need a small group of the right people, the ones who can open doors, close deals, and propel your business forward.

So stop worrying about how many people you're connected with. Start focusing on the ones that matter—the ones who can make things happen.

Because at the end of the day, it's not about having a room full of the wrong people.

It's about building a network that drives success. *That* is how you win in sales.

Chapter 3: Visiting Exhibitions and Conferences – Always Go with a Plan

Exhibitions and conferences are the goldmines of sales. They offer you a unique opportunity — a rare chance to stand face-to-face with decision-makers, influencers, and key prospects. But here's the thing: simply showing up and hoping for the best? That's a rookie mistake.

Without a clear, strategic plan, these events can turn into a colossal waste of time and money. You'll end up wandering the halls like a lost tourist, overwhelmed by booths, flashy displays, and half-baked opportunities that lead to nowhere.

You want to be more than just another name tag in the crowd.

You want to walk out with meaningful connections, appointments on your calendar, and deals in your pipeline. And the secret to doing that? Having a plan before you even walk through the doors. This chapter will show you exactly how to prepare, how to act, and how to close at industry events like a pro.

Why Having a Plan Matters

Maximize Your ROI

Every minute you spend at a conference or exhibition is an investment of your time, energy, and money. Tickets, travel, hotel rooms, marketing materials — all of it adds up. So, if you're there without a plan, you're burning resources.

Going in with a strategy ensures that every moment you spend is driving you toward your goals, whether it's generating leads, nurturing relationships, or closing deals. This is your stage — make it count.

Stand Out from the Crowd

Exhibitions and conferences are noisy environments, crowded with competitors all fighting for attention. If you don't have a focused plan, you'll disappear into the background, just another face in the crowd.

But when you arrive prepared, with pre-scheduled meetings and a targeted agenda, you'll stand out. You'll be the one people remember — not because you handed them a business card, but because you offered value and insight that sticks.

Increase Your Chances of Closing Deals

Spontaneous conversations are nice, but they rarely lead to closed deals. When you've set up meetings with decision-makers ahead of time, those conversations become laser-focused. They're about solving problems, exploring opportunities, and moving deals forward.

The pros aren't just walking around hoping to bump into prospects — they've got meetings lined up and ready to roll.

How to Prepare for an Exhibition or Conference

Identify Your Objectives

First things first: know what you want. Before attending any exhibition or conference, you need to define your goals. What are you looking to achieve?

Whether it's generating new leads, strengthening relationships with existing clients, or gathering competitive intelligence, your objectives will dictate how you approach the event. Everything, from your schedule to your conversations, should align with those goals.

Research Attendees and Exhibitors in Advance

Preparation is the weapon of the successful salesperson. Conferences often release attendee or exhibitor lists in advance — use that to your advantage. Make a hit list of the people and companies you want to connect with, and prioritize them. This is your blueprint for action.

- **Step 1: Prioritize Key Contacts.** Who are the decision-makers you need to meet? Make a list of the top prospects, clients, partners, or influencers. These are the people who matter most to your objectives.

- **Step 2: Understand Their Needs.** Do your homework. Know what challenges they're facing and how your solution can help. When you understand their pain points, your conversations will have depth and relevance. You'll stand out because you're not there to pitch—you're there to solve.

- **Step 3: Schedule Meetings in Advance**
  Want to play in the big leagues? Then don't leave your meetings to chance. **The best deals are made by people who've already locked down their key conversations before they even arrive.** Start reaching out weeks ahead of time, whether through LinkedIn, email, or direct calls, and book time with your top prospects and partners.

- **Step 4: Reach Out Early.** Get on their radar before they're swamped. Suggest a time to meet, and give them a clear reason to connect—whether it's discussing a particular challenge or exploring how you can collaborate.

- **Step 5: Be Flexible.** Conferences are hectic. Offer multiple time slots and be willing to meet for coffee, at their booth, or during breaks. The easier you make it for them to meet, the more likely they will say "yes."

Plan Your Event Schedule

Now that you've locked in meetings, build the rest of your schedule. This isn't a vacation—it's a business opportunity. Fill your agenda with the key sessions, booths, and networking events that align with your objectives.

- **Step 1: Map Out Key Sessions.** Highlight the panels, workshops, and keynotes that offer the insights you need—whether it's market intelligence or new industry trends.

- **Step 2: Leave Room for the Unexpected.** While a structured plan is critical, don't jam-pack your schedule. Leave space for impromptu opportunities. Some of the best connections happen over spontaneous coffee chats or hallway introductions.

Perfect Your Elevator Pitch

Time is money, and at conferences, you often only have a few minutes to make an impression. That's why your elevator pitch must be razor-sharp. Focus it on solving the customer's pain point, not on just what you do.

- **Step 1: Focus on Their Needs.**
  Tailor your pitch to address the specific challenges your prospect is facing. For example: "We help manufacturers reduce downtime by 20% with our real-time monitoring solution. Let's talk about how we can optimize your production."

- **Step 2: Keep It Conversational.**
  Don't turn your pitch into a monologue. Engage them. Ask about their current processes or challenges and let the conversation evolve naturally.

Strategies for Maximizing Your Time at the Event

Leverage Networking Opportunities

Networking isn't just about collecting business cards—it's about building real relationships. Maximize every opportunity to connect, whether at formal sessions or during social events.

- **Attend Networking Events.** These are the hidden gems. Informal settings often lead to deeper conversations and better connections.

- **Engage with Exhibitors.** Take the time to walk the exhibition floor, meet new vendors, and identify potential partnerships.

Take Notes and Follow Up Quickly

Don't rely on memory—after each meeting, jot down key points and action items. Then, follow up within 48 hours to keep the momentum going.

Deals are closed in the follow-up, not the first conversation.

Conclusion: Attending Conferences with Purpose

Exhibitions and conferences are more than just gatherings — they're high-stakes opportunities to generate leads, build relationships, and close deals.

But to win, you need more than just a presence — you need a plan.

When you approach these events with clear objectives, a solid game plan, and the discipline to execute, you won't just be another face in the crowd. You'll be the person everyone remembers. And most importantly — you'll leave with results.

Chapter 4: Why Inbound Leads Are Good, But Targeted Outbound Leads Are Better

Let's be real—*inbound leads* often feel like the golden ticket in sales.

Potential customers come to you, expressing interest in your product, as if they've already rolled out the red carpet for a deal.

It's easy to think that this is as good as it gets. **But here's the truth that separates the top 1% of closers from the rest:** inbound leads aren't always the decision-makers. They're often lower-level employees who are great at opening the door but don't have the keys to the kingdom.

If you want to close big deals with speed and precision, you can't just wait around for the right person to come knocking.

That's where *targeted outbound* sales come into play. Outbound allows you to skip the line and speak directly to the executives who have the authority—and the budget—to say "yes."

The Benefits of Inbound Leads

Inbound Leads Show Initial Interest

There's no denying that inbound leads have value.

The beauty of them is that they come to you with a degree of *self-qualification*. When someone downloads your whitepaper or requests a demo, they're already signaling interest. That's a nice head start—you don't have to convince them to care.

For instance, when a shop floor manager stumbles across your solution and reaches out, it's because they've identified a specific pain point. **That gets your foot in the door.** But remember, that manager can't sign the contract—that's where the challenge starts.

Quicker to Initiate Conversations

Engaging an inbound lead is easier—they're already familiar with your brand, so you can skip the introductory dance. They've done part of the work for you by reaching out, which speeds up those early stages like booking a call or setting up a demo.

Less Time Spent Prospecting

Inbound leads mean you spend less time prospecting, which is great for keeping a steady flow of potential customers coming in. The problem? These leads vary in quality.

And as you've probably experienced, **most inbound leads come from people with no real buying power**. So, while they save you time upfront, they often require a lot more effort later to close a deal.

The Limitations of Inbound Leads from the Shop Floor

Inbound Leads Often Come from Non-Decision-Makers

Here's the catch with inbound: most leads come from people who don't have the authority to move the needle. Sure, the shop floor supervisor sees the value in your solution, but they're not writing the checks.

You're left to navigate the organization, trying to inch your way up to the person who *can* make decisions—if you can even get there.

High Effort to Involve Budget Owners

Now you've got to turn your shop floor contact into your internal champion. This often involves coaching them on how to sell your solution to their boss—a Director of Operations, VP, or even the CFO. It's not impossible, but it's a heavy lift.

You're essentially doing two sales jobs: selling your solution and teaching your contact how to sell it up the chain.

No Direct Access to Decision-Makers

You're playing a game of telephone. And the farther you are from the real decision-maker, the more diluted your message becomes. You're relying on your contact to sell your product to their boss, and they're probably not delivering the pitch with the same fire that you would.

Longer Sales Cycles and Higher Friction

All of this adds friction to the sales process. What could've been a direct conversation with the budget holder now becomes a drawn-out saga of escalation, internal discussions, and delayed responses. The longer the cycle, the more chances for the deal to stall—or worse, disappear altogether.

Why Targeted Outbound Leads Are Better

Outbound Lets You Target Decision-Makers Directly

Here's where outbound shines. With outbound, you get to go straight to the top. No waiting for the right person to stumble upon your website—you can proactively target the key decision-makers who *actually* have the authority to make things happen.

Think about it. Instead of hoping a shop floor manager champions your product, you're reaching out directly to the VP of Operations, CFO, or CEO with a message that speaks to their big-picture goals.

Shorter Time to Engage Key Stakeholders

Outbound eliminates the middlemen. When you target the right decision-makers, you're cutting straight to the chase. You're having the conversations that matter with the people who can say "yes" or "no" on the spot. No more waiting for your shop floor contact to escalate the conversation internally—you've already reached the top.

Tailored Messaging to Business Objectives

With outbound, you're in control of the narrative. You can craft a message specifically for that decision-maker, addressing their high-level business objectives, not just the technical features of your product.

Whether it's cutting costs, increasing efficiency, or driving revenue, your message speaks to their bottom line, which resonates more with executives than a generic product pitch ever will.

For example, a targeted email to the CFO could focus on the financial benefits of your solution: "Our technology has reduced operational costs by 15% for manufacturers like yours over the past three years." That's the kind of language that gets attention from the top.

Predictable and Scalable Pipeline Growth

Unlike inbound, where you're at the mercy of random visitors, outbound sales is a *predictable machine*. You set the target, you choose the decision-makers, and you control how many people you reach.

If you know your conversion rates, you can scale outbound efforts and forecast results with precision.

If 1 out of every 10 cold calls to a VP leads to a meeting, and 1 out of every 3 meetings closes a deal, then your outbound pipeline is not just predictable — it's scalable. You're the one driving the process, not waiting for leads to come in.

Best Practices for Targeted Outbound Sales

Define Your Ideal Customer Profile (ICP)

The first step to any successful outbound strategy is knowing exactly who you're targeting. Identify the industry, company size, and specific decision-makers who are most likely to benefit from your solution. By defining your Ideal Customer Profile (ICP), you're not just cold-calling anyone — you're hitting the right targets with laser focus.

Personalize Your Outreach

Generic outreach is dead. To grab the attention of a CEO or VP, your message needs to be personal and relevant. Show them you've done your homework. Speak directly to their challenges and how your solution fits into their world. For example: "I see your company is expanding operations — our platform can help you scale while cutting operational costs by 20%."

Use a Multi-Channel Approach

Outbound isn't just about calls or emails. It's about engaging decision-makers wherever they are—LinkedIn, social media, even direct mail for high-value prospects. By showing up on multiple channels, you increase your chances of making a connection and opening a conversation.

Follow Up Diligently

Decision-makers are busy, and they're not always going to respond to your first message. But persistence pays off. Follow up with value—whether it's a case study, a relevant article, or an offer to demo your product. Each interaction should build on the last, pushing the conversation forward.

Conclusion: The Power of Targeted Outbound Leads

Inbound leads are great, but they often don't come from the people who matter most in the buying process. To close bigger deals faster, targeted outbound sales are the key. With outbound, you're reaching the decision-makers directly, shortening sales cycles, and controlling your pipeline.

You're not waiting for business to come to you—you're taking it to them. And that's how you close more deals, faster, with less friction.

Chapter 5:
Why Pipeline Is Key and Why Many Sales Reps Confuse the Funnel with the Pipeline

Every top-tier salesperson knows one thing: without a solid *pipeline*, you're shooting blind. It's the fuel that drives your revenue engine, keeps you sharp, and gets you across the finish line to hit those targets.

But here's the problem—too many sales reps confuse two very different concepts: the *sales funnel* and the *sales pipeline*.

Mixing these two up can lead to some major mismanagement of opportunities and, even worse, sets you up for missed quotas and shattered expectations. If you think a full funnel is the answer, but you neglect the health of your pipeline, you're in for a rude awakening.

In this chapter, we'll break down the fundamental differences between the sales funnel and the sales pipeline.

You'll learn why the *pipeline* is your real secret weapon for consistent success and how to avoid the common traps that reps fall into when they over-rely on the funnel.

The Difference Between a Sales Funnel and a Sales Pipeline

What Is a Sales Funnel?

The *sales funnel* is all about the *customer's journey* — from the moment they first hear about your product, right down to the decision to buy. It's called a funnel for a reason: a whole lot of prospects start at the top, but only a few make it through each stage to the very bottom, where the deal closes.

The funnel is customer-centric. It tracks how many leads move from being just aware of your product to becoming buyers.

Key Stages of a Sales Funnel:

- **Awareness:** Prospects first learn about your product or service.
- **Interest:** Prospects engage with your brand, maybe reading content or attending a webinar.
- **Consideration:** They start comparing you to other solutions.
- **Intent:** They show clear buying signals, like requesting a demo or quote.
- **Purchase:** They've made their decision and become a paying customer.

Marketing departments love funnels because they tell you how well you're capturing attention and nurturing prospects. But here's the kicker—it doesn't show you what *you*, the salesperson, are doing to close the deal. That's where the pipeline comes in.

What Is a Sales Pipeline?

Now let's talk about the *sales pipeline*, which is all about **you**. The pipeline represents the actions you take, step by step, to move deals from prospect to customer. It's your roadmap. If the funnel is what the customer is doing, the pipeline is what *you* are doing to make sure that deal crosses the finish line.

The pipeline is action-driven, and every stage is about what *you* need to do to push the deal forward—whether it's making that first call, sending out a proposal, or negotiating terms.

Key Stages of a Sales Pipeline:

- **Lead Generation:** Finding your potential customers.
- **Qualification:** Making sure they have the need, budget, and authority to make a purchase.
- **Proposal/Offer:** Putting your solution in front of them with a formal offer.
- **Negotiation:** Overcoming objections and fine-tuning the details.
- **Closing:** Getting that signature and sealing the deal.

Funnel vs. Pipeline: The Key Distinctions

- **Customer-Centric vs. Sales-Centric:** The funnel is about the customer's journey, while the pipeline is focused on *your actions* to drive the deal forward.
- **Stages of Engagement vs. Stages of Action:** The funnel tracks how the customer feels about you, while the pipeline tracks what you're doing to move them closer to a decision.
- **Top-Down vs. Linear:** The funnel narrows as leads drop out, but the pipeline is a linear path—either you're advancing the deal, or you're not.

Why Many Sales Reps Confuse the Funnel with a Pipeline

Mistaking Interest for Progress

Here's where sales reps often go wrong—they confuse *interest* at the top of the funnel with actual *progress* through the pipeline.

Just because someone downloads a whitepaper or attends a webinar doesn't mean they're ready to buy. That's an *engagement*, not a qualified lead.

Think about it: you could have hundreds of prospects in the "interest" phase, but if none of them are budget-holders or decision-makers, you're not moving deals through your pipeline.

Example:
A prospect downloading an eBook doesn't mean they're buying. That's just the "interest" phase in the funnel. They're not a pipeline opportunity until they've shown buying intent, and you've qualified them.

Overloading the Funnel but Neglecting Pipeline Health

A classic mistake is overloading the top of the funnel with unqualified leads while ignoring the quality of your pipeline. You might feel good about a jam-packed funnel, but what does that really mean if those leads aren't converting? It's like piling up ingredients without cooking anything.

A healthy *pipeline* is full of **qualified** leads who are moving through each stage. It's not about having a huge number of leads at the top — it's about having the right opportunities progressing toward the close.

Ignoring Critical Pipeline Metrics

Another pitfall? Ignoring the key metrics that determine whether your pipeline is healthy. Too many reps only focus on how many leads they've got in the funnel, but they're not looking at how quickly those deals are moving or what percentage are converting.

- **Pipeline Velocity:** How fast deals are moving from one stage to the next.
- **Conversion Rates:** How many leads make it from one stage of the pipeline to the next.
- **Pipeline Value:** The total value of the deals in your pipeline, adjusted for probability of close.

Without these metrics, you could be working a ton of deals that are stalled and have no real chance of closing, leading to bad forecasts and missed quotas.

Focusing on Activity Instead of Pipeline Progress

Here's another trap: confusing activity with real progress. Sure, sending out emails and making calls looks good on the surface, but is it moving the deal forward?

Reps often mistake *being busy* for being effective. You might have sent 50 follow-up emails, but if none of those leads advance, you're stuck in the same place.

Example:
You're sending follow-up emails like clockwork, but the prospect isn't moving past the "qualification" stage. Your pipeline is clogged, and unless you get them advancing, all that activity is wasted energy.

Why Your Pipeline Is the Key to Success

Accurate Sales Forecasting

Your pipeline is the foundation for predicting future revenue. By tracking where each deal is in the process and the likelihood it will close, you can accurately forecast your sales. And when you forecast correctly, you hit your targets and build trust with leadership.
Without a healthy, well-managed pipeline, your forecasts are nothing but guesswork.

Pipeline Management Helps You Prioritize

A well-structured pipeline lets you focus your time on the deals that matter most. If you know where each deal is in the process, you can direct your energy to the ones closest to closing or those that need immediate attention.

Example:
If you've got a deal in the negotiation phase, it's going to need more attention than one still in qualification.

By managing your pipeline, you're always working on the deals with the highest potential for closing.

Preventing Pipeline Stagnation

Deals can stall. And without regular pipeline management, they can sit in the same stage for weeks, even months. But a well-monitored pipeline allows you to spot bottlenecks and take action—whether that's moving the deal forward or disqualifying it altogether.

Focus on Quality Over Quantity

A large funnel might look impressive, but it's the *quality* of your pipeline that makes or breaks your success. You'd rather have a lean pipeline filled with qualified, high-potential deals than a bloated pipeline full of leads that aren't going anywhere.

How to Build and Maintain a Healthy Sales Pipeline

Qualify Leads Early and Thoroughly

Qualify leads before advancing them in your pipeline. This keeps unqualified opportunities from clogging your system. Use methods like BANT (Budget, Authority, Need, Timeline) to ensure only serious prospects make it into your pipeline.

Regularly Review and Update Your Pipeline

Pipeline management is a daily task. You should be reviewing it regularly—at least weekly—to make sure deals are advancing. If they're not, it's time to either push them forward or cut them loose.

Focus on Moving Deals Forward

Every stage in the pipeline represents an action. Whether it's booking a demo, sending a proposal, or negotiating terms, always have a goal in mind. Keep deals moving, and never let them get stuck in limbo.

Conclusion: Understand the Difference and Focus on the Pipeline

Don't confuse the sales funnel with your pipeline. The funnel is a good indicator of interest, but it's the pipeline that drives your success.

A strong pipeline helps you prioritize, forecast accurately, and close more deals. It's not about how many leads you have—it's about how well you're moving those leads toward the finish line.

If you want to hit your targets consistently, invest in your pipeline, keep it healthy, and always focus on progress.

A full funnel is nice, but a strong pipeline is what gets the deal done.

Chapter 6:

Create a Pitch That Brings Value to Your Customers – Don't Sell Features, Sell Value!

One of the biggest pitfalls in sales is focusing too much on features—rattling off specs, diving into technical details, and throwing jargon at your prospect. Sure, it might sound impressive, but here's the hard truth: *customers don't buy features.*

They buy *solutions* to their problems, *improvements* to their operations, and *ways to make their lives easier.*

If you want to win in sales, you need to shift the conversation from "what does my product do?" to "what can my product do for *you*?" It's not about listing features— it's about showing value, addressing pain points, and aligning with your customer's goals.
In this chapter, we'll break down how to craft a pitch that's value-driven and customer-focused.

We'll go from understanding your customer's needs to delivering a pitch that makes them see your solution as a game-changer.

Know Your Customer's Pain Points

Before you can create a pitch that screams value, you need to *truly understand* what your customer cares about. It's not just about selling your product—it's about solving their problems. To sell value, you need to get inside their world, understand their pain points, and figure out how your solution makes those problems disappear.

Step 1: Research the Customer

Start by diving deep into your customer's industry, business model, and competitive landscape. What challenges are they facing in the market right now? What are their customers demanding? What's keeping them up at night?
For example, if you're selling a SaaS solution to a manufacturing company, don't just talk about cloud infrastructure or integration. Instead, frame your pitch around how your software helps them reduce production downtime or eliminate inefficiencies in their workflow.

Step 2: Ask the Right Questions

To uncover your customer's true pain points, ask open-ended questions that guide the conversation toward their challenges and goals. This transforms your interaction from a sales pitch to a consultative conversation, showing you're more interested in *their* success than in pushing your product.

Try questions like:
- "What's the biggest challenge your team is currently dealing with?"
- "How do these challenges impact your overall business performance?"
- "If you could solve one operational problem, what would that look like?"

Their answers will serve as your roadmap, allowing you to craft a pitch that directly addresses what matters most to them.

Translate Features into Benefits

Once you've mapped out your customer's pain points, it's time to connect the dots between your product's features and the *benefits* they'll bring. Features tell your customer *what* your product does—benefits show them *how* it solves their problems.

Let's say you're selling a SaaS platform that streamlines operations. One of the features might be real-time data analytics. Instead of diving into the technical specs, translate that feature into something meaningful: "Real-time analytics means your team can make data-driven decisions faster, reducing costly delays and improving operational efficiency."

Here's how to turn features into value-packed benefits:

- **Feature:** "Our platform automates task management across multiple teams." **Benefit:** "With automated task management, your teams will save time and reduce errors, improving overall productivity by 15%."

- **Feature:** "Our software integrates with all your existing tools." **Benefit:** "Seamless integration means your team can continue working with the tools they already know, without the learning curve or downtime."

- **Feature:** "We offer 24/7 customer support." **Benefit:** "With round-the-clock support, you'll never worry about unexpected downtime or technical issues slowing down your operations."

The key? Always tie the feature back to the customer's pain points. How will this specific feature make their lives easier, improve efficiency, or drive revenue? Make it personal

Focus on ROI (Return on Investment)

One of the most compelling ways to show value is by demonstrating the *return on investment* (ROI) your solution delivers. Customers don't just want to hear about improvements—they want to know the bottom-line impact. If your product saves time, money, or increases revenue, *quantify it*. Give them numbers.

For example, if your SaaS solution reduces operational downtime, don't just say that. Frame it as: "By reducing downtime by 10%, you'll save $100,000 annually in labor costs."

Here's how to highlight ROI in your pitch:

Time Savings: Show how your solution reduces time spent on specific tasks, leading to cost savings and higher efficiency.
"With our SaaS platform, your team can reduce reporting time by 50%, which translates into a 20% productivity increase across your entire department."

Cost Savings: Explain how your solution will save them money in the long run by reducing operational costs, minimizing errors, or optimizing resource use.
"By using our platform, you'll cut down on IT expenses by 25%, saving over $50,000 annually."

Revenue Growth: Show how your solution can help them grow their business—whether through capturing more leads, improving customer satisfaction, or driving sales.
"Our solution increases lead capture by 15%, which could potentially grow your annual revenue by $200,000."

ROI-focused pitches turn your solution into a financial no-brainer.

Tell a Story

Humans connect with stories. Storytelling in sales brings your value proposition to life—it gives your customer a tangible example of how your solution has worked for others. When you tell a story that relates to your customer's situation, you make it easier for them to visualize themselves benefiting in the same way.

For example:
"One of our clients in the SaaS market was dealing with scattered data across multiple systems, causing inefficiencies that slowed down their growth. After implementing our platform, they were able to consolidate all their data streams, automate reporting, and reduce their IT costs by 30%. Within six months, they saw a 25% improvement in operational efficiency and saved over $100,000 in costs."

That story does more than explain—it *proves* that your solution works. It provides social proof that you're not just selling potential—you're delivering results.

Conclusion: Selling Value, Not Features

Your customers aren't interested in hearing about the bells and whistles of your product.

They want to know *how* your solution will make a difference to *their* business. Selling value means focusing on what your solution can do for them—how it will improve efficiency, solve problems, and deliver ROI.

By understanding your customer's pain points, translating features into benefits, focusing on measurable outcomes, and telling powerful stories, you can craft a pitch that resonates on a deeper level.

**Remember: customers don't buy products.
They buy the *value* those products bring to their business.**

Focus on delivering that value, and you'll not only close more deals—you'll build lasting, meaningful relationships with your customers.

Chapter 7:

Gorillas Don't Bite! – Why It's Important to Talk to the Person with Power

It's easy to feel nervous about approaching high-level decision-makers—the CEOs, VPs, Directors, or C-suite executives who hold the ultimate power to say "yes" or "no" to your deal.

These "big gorillas" can seem intimidating, and the fear of rejection, or the belief that you might not be important enough to get their attention, can be overwhelming.

But here's the thing: **these** are the **exact people you need to be talking to**.

Why? Because decision-makers have the authority to make decisions quickly, push deals forward, and commit resources. If you spend your time talking to people who lack the power to make decisions, you'll likely end up in endless conversations that lead nowhere.

This chapter will walk you through why it's crucial to speak directly to the person with power, how to approach them confidently, and what strategies you can use to leave a lasting impression.

Why Decision-Makers Matter

The Gatekeepers vs. The Decision-Makers

Many sales reps fall into the trap of engaging gatekeepers—mid-level managers, department heads, or procurement officers—who don't have the final authority to make decisions.

While these individuals can provide valuable insights and might influence the decision-making process, they lack the power to close the deal.

Decision-makers, however, have the authority to say "yes" or "no." They're the ones who can sign contracts, allocate budgets, and approve partnerships. If you're pitching to someone who doesn't have that power, even if they love your solution, they'll still need to get approval from someone above them, which can slow the process, dilute your message, or worse—your pitch may lose momentum before it even reaches the decision-maker.

Speed Up the Sales Process

Talking directly to the person in power cuts through the layers of decision-making that can slow down the sales process. High-level executives tend to be more decisive, especially if they see the value in your offer. **When you're engaging with the "big gorilla," you're speaking to someone with the authority to make things happen.**

For example, a CEO can set strategic priorities, a CFO can approve a budget, and a VP of Sales can allocate resources. These individuals aren't bogged down by the internal delays that can stifle decisions at lower levels.

When you engage with them directly, you can fast-track conversations and ensure your pitch reaches the right person.

Align with Business Goals

High-level decision-makers have a wide-angle view of the business. They understand the company's strategic goals, financial priorities, and long-term vision.

This means they're not just looking for a solution that solves a department's issue—they want something that drives the company forward.

When you pitch to a decision-maker, your message must align with their strategic objectives. They're thinking bigger than saving money in one area; they want to know how your solution impacts growth, profitability, or competitive advantage.

This is why talking to the person with power is so important—they're focused on how your solution fits into the bigger picture.

How to Approach the Big Gorilla with Confidence

Talking to top-tier executives may seem daunting, but with the right approach, you can turn it into a game-changing opportunity. Here are key strategies to help you engage with decision-makers confidently and effectively.

1. Do Your Homework

Before reaching out to an executive, **preparation is key**. Executives have no patience for vague pitches. You need to understand their business, industry, and specific pain points.

Do thorough research on:
- Recent news about their company, including any new initiatives, acquisitions, or market challenges.
- Their company's financial performance, if publicly available.
- The specific responsibilities of the executive you're contacting (e.g., the CEO might care about market expansion, while the CFO is focused on cost management).
- The strategic goals or pain points your SaaS solution addresses.

The more you know about their business, the more personalized and relevant your pitch will be. Executives respond well to someone who understands their world and offers something that matters to them.

2. Lead with Value

When you finally get the chance to speak to a decision-maker, cut straight to the value. **Lead with the problem you solve and the benefit it brings to their organization.**

Don't waste time listing all your features. Instead, focus on the high-level benefits and business impact.

For example, if you're talking to the CEO of a SaaS company, you could say: "From our research, we understand that optimizing customer acquisition is critical for your company's growth. Our SaaS solution can help you reduce customer churn by 15%, which could increase your annual revenue by $2 million. I'd love to discuss how we can help you achieve that."

This approach immediately demonstrates that you understand their priorities and can deliver value that aligns with their business goals.

3. Be Direct and Concise

Executives are short on time. Be clear and concise in your communication. Whether in an email or a meeting, get to the point quickly. Explain why you're reaching out, what you offer, and why it matters to them.

Here's an example of an effective email:

"Dear [Name],

I noticed that your company is expanding into new markets, and I believe our SaaS solution could help optimize your customer acquisition during this growth.

We recently helped a similar company increase acquisition by 20%, driving an additional $5 million in annual revenue.

I'd love to schedule a brief meeting to discuss how we can help you achieve similar results. Let me know a convenient time for you."

This message shows the value you bring, backs it up with proof, and makes it easy for them to say "yes" to a conversation.

4. Speak Their Language

Different decision-makers have different priorities. A CEO is focused on strategy and growth, while a CFO zeroes in on cost control and financial metrics. Tailor your pitch to the person you're speaking to, using the language and metrics that matter to them.

When speaking to a CFO, highlight ROI, cost savings, and financial impact. For a VP of Sales, focus on how your SaaS solution can improve sales performance or drive revenue.

Speaking their language makes it easier for them to see the value in what you're offering.

5. Build Relationships

Even though decision-makers are busy, they value relationships. Don't view your interaction as a one-off transaction.

If you can build a strong relationship, you're not only more likely to close the current deal, but you'll also create opportunities for future business.

Follow up regularly, offer valuable insights, and continue to engage even after the sale. Decision-makers appreciate partners who help them succeed long-term, not just vendors who disappear after the contract is signed.

Conclusion: Face the Big Gorilla Head-On

It's natural to feel intimidated by the big gorilla — the executive with all the power — because the stakes are high.

But if you want to close significant deals and make real progress, you have to engage with the person who has the authority to say "yes."

By preparing thoroughly, leading with value, and speaking the language of decision-makers, you can confidently approach the key players in your industry and build lasting relationships that lead to success. Remember, decision-makers are looking for solutions that align with their strategic goals and deliver tangible impact.

Don't be afraid to face them head-on — be confident, concise, and always focused on the value you bring to their business.

Chapter 8:
Sweep the Floor but Always Have an Eye on the Ceiling – Balancing Shop Floor Insights and Decision-Maker Priorities

When crafting a sales strategy, the natural inclination is to focus squarely on decision-makers and budget owners—the ones at the top of the organizational hierarchy who can sign contracts and release funds.

While gaining buy-in from these key players is essential, there's another critical group that often holds the keys to your long-term success: the frontline workers, supervisors, and technicians who will interact with your solution every day.

Ignoring this group is a mistake. They may not control the budget, but they hold valuable insights into day-to-day operations and can provide feedback on how your solution will function in real-world conditions.

What's more, these shop-floor workers can become powerful internal advocates, persuading their higher-ups to greenlight your solution.

In this chapter, we'll dive into why engaging with the shop floor is crucial, how to incorporate their insights while keeping decision-makers in mind, and how to use this dual perspective to create a sales pitch that resonates with everyone from the ground up.

Why the Shop Floor Matters

1. They're the Frontline Users

No matter how innovative your SaaS solution may be, if it doesn't work for the people on the ground, it won't succeed. The shop floor workers, operators, and supervisors are the ones who deal with the processes, tools, and technology day in and day out.

They know where the real-world challenges, inefficiencies, and bottlenecks are — and they're often the first to spot whether your solution will improve their workflows.

By engaging with them, you gain a much deeper understanding of how your solution can best be applied to solve their specific problems. These insights can be the difference between selling a product that works in theory and one that drives actual, measurable improvements — whether it's reducing downtime, streamlining operations, or boosting productivity.

2. They Can Be Your Champions

One of the most overlooked aspects of selling to large organizations is the power of internal advocacy. While shop floor workers may not have the final say, they often wield considerable influence over the decision-makers. If they see real value in your solution, they can become strong advocates within their organization, helping to push your deal forward.

For example, let's say you're offering a SaaS platform to streamline asset management. If the frontline workers see how your solution can save them hours each day and reduce frustration, they'll start talking about it to their supervisors.

Those supervisors might bring it up to their managers, and suddenly, you have an entire department on your side when you pitch to the budget holder.

3. They Provide Practical Insights

While decision-makers focus on strategy, vision, and financials, they often lack detailed knowledge of what happens on the shop floor. The people working on the ground can give you hands-on, practical feedback about the challenges they face and whether your solution will make a meaningful difference.

Engaging with them during the sales process allows you to refine your pitch and product offering. They might point out implementation issues or suggest features that would make your solution more effective. This kind of insight not only helps you tailor your proposal to better meet the needs of the organization but also shows decision-makers that you've done your homework and understand the full scope of their operational challenges.

Balancing the Two Audiences: Shop Floor and Decision Maker

1. Engage Shop Floor Workers Without Bypassing the Decision-Maker

While it's crucial to involve shop-floor workers, you mustn't bypass the decision-makers or budget holders. Doing so can create tension or make it seem like you're ignoring the hierarchy, which can backfire.

The key is to strike a balance.

- **Work with Management**: When engaging with frontline workers, ensure the decision-makers are informed and involved. For example, you could ask for permission to speak with operational staff, positioning it as a way to gather insights that will help the solution succeed across the organization.

- **Frame the Conversation**: When you speak with shop-floor workers, emphasize that your goal is to understand how the solution will benefit them directly. Explain that their feedback is invaluable and that you're committed to ensuring the solution works for everyone. This builds trust and rapport without undermining management.

- **Relay Their Feedback**: Once you've gathered insights from the shop floor, present those findings to decision-makers in a way that strengthens your pitch. For example, if you learn that a current system is causing downtime or confusion, you can highlight this to the decision-maker as evidence of why your SaaS solution is a better fit.

2. Align Shop Floor Concerns with Strategic Goals

While shop floor workers are focused on solving day-to-day challenges, decision-makers are concerned with broader strategic goals — profitability, scalability, and growth. The key to a successful pitch is to align these practical concerns with the company's bigger objectives.

For instance, imagine you're selling a SaaS solution for tracking workflows. The shop floor workers are interested in how it helps them finish tasks more efficiently, while the CFO is focused on reducing operational costs.

To bridge the two perspectives, you might say:

"After speaking with your team, we identified that it takes about 20 minutes per shift to complete certain manual tasks, leading to operational delays. With our SaaS platform, this time can be reduced by 80%, improving productivity and saving your company an estimated $100,000 annually in labor costs."

This approach connects the practical benefits that resonate with shop floor workers to the financial goals of the decision-maker.

3. Turn Feedback Into a Stronger Pitch

Once you've gathered feedback from both the shop floor and the decision-makers, you can craft a more powerful pitch that shows you understand the company's needs from all angles. This demonstrates that you've done your research and can offer a well-rounded solution.

For example, if frontline workers have mentioned that their current system has frequent technical issues that slow them down, you can use that insight in your pitch to the decision-maker:

"Your team has highlighted that the current system frequently crashes, causing workflow disruptions. Our SaaS platform not only resolves those technical issues but also includes 24/7 support, ensuring that downtime is minimized, which directly contributes to your goal of increasing efficiency and reducing costs."

The Role of the Budget Owner and Decision Maker in the Process

While shop-floor feedback is crucial, it's the budget owner and decision-maker who have the final say. Always keep them at the forefront of your process, ensuring that you're addressing their priorities—ROI, strategic alignment, and long-term value.

Here's how to keep them engaged:

- **Provide Regular Updates**: After gathering feedback from the shop floor, update the decision-makers regularly. Show them how these insights are shaping your proposal and solution.

- **Connect the Dots**: Explain how the shop-floor feedback supports the business case. Show how solving operational issues aligns with larger business objectives.

- **Emphasize ROI**: Always return to the financials. Decision-makers need to see that your solution not only fixes operational problems but also delivers measurable returns, such as cost savings, increased efficiency, or revenue growth.

Conclusion: Bridging the Gap Between the Shop Floor and the Decision-Maker

In sales, it's essential to engage with both the people on the shop floor and the higher-ups who control the budget.

Each group provides a unique perspective — shop-floor workers offer real-world insights into how your solution will work in practice, while decision-makers focus on its broader strategic and financial impact.

By gathering insights from both groups, aligning them with the company's goals, and delivering an ROI-focused pitch to decision-makers, you'll position yourself as a trusted advisor who understands the business from top to bottom.

This approach not only increases the likelihood of closing the deal but also sets the stage for long-term success — for both you and your customer.

Chapter 9: Understanding the Customer – What Keeps Them Awake at Night

If you want to truly succeed, you need to understand your customer beyond the surface. It's not enough to know what product they sell or the industry they're in—you need to dive deeper.

You must empathize with their pain points, get inside their challenges, and align your solution with their long-term goals. So, what's keeping them awake at night? What hurdles stand between them and their success, and how can your solution be the one that removes those obstacles?

In this chapter, we'll explore the importance of gaining a deep understanding of your customer's business, how to uncover the core problems that matter most to them, and how to position your product or service as the solution to their most pressing issues.

We'll also cover how you can help them reduce costs, grow their revenue, and even operate more sustainably—because in today's fast-paced market, being able to deliver on all three is a game-changer.

Why Understanding the Customer Is Critical

1. It Builds Trust and Credibility

If you want to stand out as more than just another salesperson, you have to show that you're invested in your customer's success. When you take the time to really understand their business, it's clear that you're not just pushing a product—you're offering a tailored solution. Customers trust those who understand their world, recognize their pain points, and speak their language.

This level of understanding also positions you as a credible source. If you can talk about industry trends, market challenges, and their specific business problems with insight, you become a *trusted advisor*, not just another vendor. That trust is the tipping point between a closed deal and a missed opportunity.

2. It Helps You Tailor Your Value Proposition

Every business is unique. What works for one company won't necessarily work for another. When you understand your customer's business on a deeper level, you can tailor your pitch to their specific goals and challenges. A company in manufacturing might care about reducing downtime, while a retailer might be focused on improving customer experience to drive more sales.

Tailoring your value proposition to highlight what *really* matters to the customer makes your pitch far more compelling. It shows that you've done your homework and that you're offering a solution, not just features.

3. It Provides Insight into Future Opportunities

Understanding your customer's business also opens the door to future opportunities. Businesses evolve, and the solutions that help them today may need to adapt tomorrow. When you understand their long-term goals, you can position yourself as a partner ready to help them grow, scale, and meet new challenges. This not only increases your chances of upselling or cross-selling but also positions you as an ongoing partner in their success, not just a one-time vendor.

What Keeps Your Customer Awake at Night?

1. Financial Pressure: Reducing Costs and Improving Profitability

For almost every business, financial pressure is top of mind. Whether it's controlling costs, improving margins, or avoiding unnecessary expenses, decision-makers are always thinking about the bottom line. In manufacturing, downtime can bleed money. In retail, overhead costs can be crushing. Regardless of the industry, if your solution doesn't address their financial pain points, you're missing the mark.

When talking to your customer, ask questions that reveal their financial worries:

- "What are your biggest operational costs, and where do you think improvements could be made?"

- "Are there inefficiencies in your current process that are impacting your bottom line?"

- "How much of a priority is cost reduction for your business right now?"

Once you understand their financial pressures, you can tailor your pitch to show how your product can help reduce costs and improve profitability. If you're selling SaaS, for example, emphasize how automation can save time, reduce labor costs, and streamline processes—all of which improve their financial outlook.

2. Growth Challenges: Increasing Sales and Expanding Market Reach

Growth is the ultimate goal for any company—whether it's increasing sales, expanding into new markets, or boosting customer retention. But growth is never easy, and the path is often filled with roadblocks. Companies are always trying to figure out how to get bigger, faster, and better.

If your solution can help drive sales or open up new market opportunities, you're tapping into one of the biggest concerns your customer has.

To uncover these growth-related pain points, ask:

- "What are your current growth goals, and what's standing in the way of achieving them?"

- "Are there bottlenecks in your sales process that are slowing down your growth?"

- "How are you approaching market expansion, and what challenges are you facing?"

Once you know what's keeping them from growing, position your solution as the growth engine they need. If you sell sales software, talk about how it can boost conversion rates.

If it's a marketing tool, show how it can help them expand into new markets and capture more customers.

3. Sustainability and Social Responsibility

Sustainability isn't just a buzzword anymore—it's become a business necessity. Consumers are demanding more accountability from the companies they buy from, and that pressure is forcing businesses to operate in more eco-friendly, socially responsible ways. Businesses want to reduce their environmental footprint, waste less, and do more good. If you understand that sustainability is a priority for your customer, you can use that to your advantage in your pitch.

Ask questions that uncover their sustainability goals:

- "What steps are you currently taking to reduce your environmental impact?"

- "Are there areas in your operations where you think sustainability could be improved?"

- "How important is sustainability to your brand and customer relationships?"

If your SaaS solution can help reduce energy consumption, minimize waste, or promote more sustainable practices, highlight those benefits. Sustainability isn't just a value-add—it's a growing business imperative.

How to Help Your Customer Reduce Costs, Make Better Sales, or Be More Sustainable

1. Help Reduce Costs with Efficient Solutions

Nothing gets a decision-maker's attention like a clear path to cost savings. If you can show how your solution reduces costs, you've already won half the battle. Whether it's automating processes, streamlining workflows, or eliminating inefficiencies, your product needs to demonstrate measurable financial impact.

For example:

- "Our solution can reduce your operational downtime by 30%, translating to $200,000 in annual savings."

- "By automating this process, you'll reduce labor costs by 15%, saving $50,000 per year."

- Show them the data. Decision-makers want to know exactly how your solution impacts the bottom line.

2. Help Increase Sales by Supporting Growth

Your customer wants to grow, and your solution should be positioned as the key to unlocking that growth. Whether it's expanding into new markets, improving sales performance, or driving more revenue from existing customers, make sure your product is seen as a growth driver.

For example:

- "By implementing our solution, your sales team will increase lead conversion by 25%, driving an additional $500,000 in revenue annually."

- "Our platform will streamline your marketing efforts, allowing you to expand into new markets and capture a larger share of your customer base."

- Align your solution with their growth objectives and show how you're the key to getting there faster.

3. Promote Sustainability with Eco-Friendly Solutions

If sustainability is one of their core goals, position your solution as both a smart business decision and an environmentally responsible one. Show how your SaaS product can reduce waste, lower energy consumption, or help them operate more responsibly.

For example:

- "Our software reduces your energy consumption by 40%, helping you meet your sustainability targets."

- "By digitizing this process, you'll cut paper waste by 80%, aligning with your company's eco-friendly initiatives."

When your solution hits both their financial and sustainability goals, you're offering them a win-win.

Conclusion: Solving the Problems That Matter Most

At the end of the day, sales isn't just about pushing a product—it's about solving problems.

The better you understand what drives your customer, what challenges they're up against, and what keeps them awake at night, the better equipped you are to offer a solution that fits.

Ask the right questions, dig deep into their needs, and tailor your pitch to show how your product solves their most pressing problems—whether that's cutting costs, driving growth, or making their business more sustainable.

When you do this, you're not just a salesperson—you're a partner in their success.

And that's what keeps the deals rolling in.

Chapter 10:
Why BANT is the Key: How to Ensure You Have Budget, Authority, Need, and Timing (BANT) Covered

One of the most effective frameworks for qualifying prospects and maximizing your chances of closing a deal is BANT: Budget, Authority, Need, and Timing.

This framework ensures that you're targeting the right people and pursuing opportunities with a high likelihood of success. By covering BANT, you'll know if the person you're speaking with can actually say "yes" (Authority), if they have a real problem your solution can fix (Need), if they have the financial resources to buy (Budget), and if the timing is right to move forward (Timing).

Each element of BANT is crucial. Miss one, and even the most promising deals can unravel. In this chapter, we're diving deep into BANT, how to apply it in your sales process, and why it's your ticket to closing more deals efficiently.

1. Budget: Do They Have the Funds?

Understanding your prospect's budget is one of the first steps in qualifying a lead. You could have the perfect solution, but if they don't have the money to buy it, you're spinning your wheels.

How to Uncover Budget:

- **Ask Direct Questions:** The key is to inquire about budget without making it sound like all you care about is getting paid. Frame the conversation around solving their problems. Ask questions like, "Has a budget been allocated to solve this issue?" or "What's your budget range for addressing this challenge?" This approach makes the question about helping them, not about your bottom line.

- **Understand Financial Priorities:** Even if there's no formal budget yet, they may still be willing to find the money if your solution delivers enough value. Show them how your solution improves ROI, whether it's cutting costs, increasing efficiency, or boosting revenue. For example: "While you may not have a budget set aside for this, implementing our solution could reduce your downtime by 20%, saving your company $X annually."

- **Identify Financial Cycles:** Some companies may not have funds right now, but that doesn't mean they won't soon. Ask about their fiscal calendar: "When does your fiscal year end?" or "When do you typically make budgeting decisions for new initiatives?" This way, you can time your proposal for when the money is available.

How to Secure Budget:

Once you've identified the available budget (or justified the cost through clear ROI), make sure to engage the right financial stakeholders. Keep them invested with hard data and projections, showing how your solution impacts their financial goals directly.

2. Authority: Are You Talking to the Right Person?

It's not enough to have someone at a company interested in your product. You need to make sure that the person you're speaking to can actually make the purchasing decision—or at least influence it. Without Authority, you'll end up wasting time in endless meetings that go nowhere.

How to Identify Authority:

- **Ask About Decision-Making:** Early in your discussions, ask questions like, "Who's involved in the decision-making process for something like this?" or "How are decisions like this typically made in your company?" These questions reveal whether you're talking to someone who has the final say—or whether they'll need to loop in other decision-makers.

- **Look at Titles and Roles:** While job titles like CEO, VP, or Director usually indicate authority, don't rely solely on titles. Sometimes, decision-making is shared between multiple people or departments. Always verify who has the power to make the call.

- **Engage Multiple Stakeholders:** If the person you're speaking with isn't the final decision-maker, ask for an introduction to the key players. For example: "I understand that your CFO would need to weigh in on the financial aspect of this solution. Could we set up a meeting to go over those details together?"

How to Secure Authority:

Once you've identified the decision-makers, bring them into the conversation directly. This may mean setting up meetings with the CEO, CFO, or department heads. Your job is to make sure your pitch resonates with each decision-maker's unique priorities — whether it's ROI for the CFO or strategic fit for the CEO.

3. Need: Do They Have a Problem Your Solution Can Solve?

No matter how great your product is, if the prospect doesn't have a real need for it, they won't buy. Your job is to uncover that need — and tie your solution to solving it.

How to Identify Need:

- **Diagnose the Pain Points:** During your discovery phase, ask open-ended questions to find out what challenges your prospect is facing. Questions like, "What's your biggest challenge in this area?" or "What's preventing your company from reaching its goals?" can help you uncover underlying problems your solution can fix.

- **Reveal Opportunities:** Sometimes, customers don't even realize how big their problems are until you show them. Ask questions like, "Have you considered how much time is lost due to inefficiencies in your current system?" or "What would a 20% reduction in downtime mean for your business?" These types of questions make your prospect think more critically about their need and how you can help.

- **Tie the Need to Business Goals:** Always connect your solution to the customer's broader business objectives. Show how solving their immediate pain points helps them achieve their larger goals, whether that's improving efficiency, cutting costs, or driving revenue.

How to Secure Need:

Once you've identified a clear need, reframe your conversation around solving it quickly. You want to create urgency by showing the cost of inaction. For example: "Every month without this solution is costing you $X in lost productivity. The sooner we implement it, the sooner you'll start saving money."

4. Timing: Is the Timing Right?

Even if the prospect has the budget, authority, and a pressing need, if the timing isn't right, the deal won't close. Understanding when they are ready to move forward is essential.

How to Identify Timing:

- **Ask About Urgency:** Timing is all about urgency. Ask, "How urgent is solving this issue for your business?" or "What happens if you don't address this challenge within the next few months?" These questions help you gauge how quickly the prospect is ready to act.

- **Understand Their Calendar:** Many businesses operate on fiscal or budget cycles, making purchases at specific times of the year. Ask questions like, "When do you typically review new investments?" or "Are there any upcoming deadlines or projects that could affect the timing of this decision?"

- **Spot Roadblocks:** Timing can also be delayed by other priorities within the organization. Ask about potential roadblocks: "Are there any other projects or constraints that might push this decision back?"

How to Secure Timing:

Once you know the customer's timeline, adjust your sales process accordingly. If they need more time, stay engaged by offering valuable insights or content to keep the conversation going. If they're ready to move quickly, focus on speeding up the decision-making process and reinforcing the benefits of acting now.

Bringing It All Together: Using BANT to Qualify and Close Deals

Once you've covered Budget, Authority, Need, and Timing, you have a solid framework to move the deal forward and close it.

Here's a quick recap of how to bring everything together:

1. **Budget:** Ensure they have the financial resources to buy your solution. If needed, show clear ROI to justify the cost.

2. **Authority:** Make sure you're speaking with the person who can make the final decision, or get introduced to them.

3. **Need:** Uncover their most pressing challenges and show how your solution solves them.

4. **Timing:** Align your sales process with their timeline, ensuring the purchase happens when they're ready.

Conclusion: Mastering BANT for Sales Success

BANT is more than just a qualification tool — it's a roadmap for closing deals. When you master the art of qualifying prospects based on **Budget, Authority, Need, and Timing**, you avoid wasting time on dead-end leads and focus your energy on opportunities that are primed for success.

By covering these four elements, you gain a comprehensive understanding of your prospect's situation, allowing you to tailor your approach and pitch with precision.

This not only increases your chances of closing more deals but also strengthens your overall sales pipeline.

Chapter 11:

Make It Easy for Your Customer to Buy from You – Nobody Wants to Get Sold, Everyone Wants to Buy

Here's the thing about sales: nobody likes being sold to, but everyone loves buying. It's a simple yet powerful truth. The moment customers feel like they're being pressured or forced into a decision, they put up walls.

However, when the process is smooth, intuitive, and aligned with their needs, they're more than willing to buy. The magic happens when the experience is about them, not you.

In this chapter, we'll explore how you can create a frictionless, customer-focused buying process. By shifting your mindset from "selling" to "facilitating a purchase," you'll guide customers toward making decisions that feel natural, confident, and right for them.

We'll dive into eliminating friction, offering transparency, and becoming a trusted guide—so your customers feel like they're making the decision on their terms.

Why Nobody Wants to Be Sold

1. The Pressure of a Sales Pitch

When customers sense they're being "pitched" instead of consulted, walls go up. Pressure-heavy pitches make people uncomfortable, often feeling like they're more about your commission than their needs. When the buyer feels you're more interested in the deal than in genuinely solving their problems, you lose credibility.

The goal is to make sales a collaborative effort, not a high-stakes negotiation. Customers want to feel like they are in control, not being pushed into a corner. When you become the guide rather than the salesperson, you open the door for genuine relationships and trust.

2. The Shift Toward Buyer Empowerment

Today's buyers are savvier than ever. They're armed with research, reviews, comparisons, and alternatives before they even talk to you. That means they don't need you to bombard them with product info — they need you to help them make sense of the information they already have.

High-pressure sales tactics belong in the past. Modern buyers expect collaboration, transparency, and respect for their intelligence. They're looking for a process that's simple, logical, and leads them to the right solution without any manipulation.

How to Make It Easy for Your Customer to Buy from You

Simplify the Buying Process

The more complicated and confusing you make the buying process, the more likely it is that your customer will walk away. Your goal is to remove any unnecessary steps, eliminate confusion, and make it obvious how to move forward.

Step 1: Clarify the Path to Purchase

No matter how simple or complex your sales process is, the path to purchase should be crystal clear. Whether it's an online checkout or a multi-stage B2B deal, every step must be intuitive.

For example:

- Provide transparent pricing upfront.
- Eliminate legal jargon in contracts.
- Give clear instructions on next steps after a demo or consultation.

Step 2: Streamline Your Offerings

Too many options can overwhelm customers and lead to decision paralysis. Avoid bombarding them with endless product variations. Instead, streamline your offerings to focus on what solves their specific problems. Offer personalized recommendations to help them quickly see what best fits their needs. For example: "Based on what we discussed, the Professional Package covers all the features you need and would be the best fit at this stage."

Remove Friction Points

Friction points are the moments where doubt, confusion, or hesitation creep in, slowing or derailing the buying process. The less friction there is, the smoother and more enjoyable the buying experience becomes.

Step 1: Address Common Objections Early

Many customers share the same concerns: pricing, implementation, or support. Tackle these upfront to reduce resistance and build trust. For example, "Many clients worry about how quickly they can implement our solution. Our dedicated team will ensure everything is up and running in 30 days, with minimal downtime."

Step 2: Offer Easy Communication Channels

Your customers should always feel like they can reach you without hassle. Offer multiple communication options — phone, email, chat, or video — so they can choose what works best for them. When they know you're easily accessible, it lowers their stress and increases confidence in the purchase process.

Step 3: Simplify the Paperwork

Nobody likes paperwork, especially when it's filled with legal jargon and complex terms. Make contracts as simple as possible, provide plain-English explanations, and offer digital signing to make it easy to finalize the deal.

The easier it is to say "yes," the more likely they'll follow through.

Be a Trusted Guide, Not a Pushy Salesperson

Customers want to buy from someone they trust, not someone trying to close a deal at any cost. Your role is to guide them through the decision-making process with transparency and empathy.

Step 1: Focus on Their Needs

Instead of hammering away at your product features, shift the focus to their challenges and needs. Ask insightful questions that get to the heart of what they're trying to solve, and then show how your solution addresses those specific pain points. For example, "It sounds like reducing downtime is your biggest concern. Let's walk through how our platform can specifically help with that."

Step 2: Empower the Customer to Decide

Instead of pushing for a close, give them the tools and space to make their own informed decision. Provide data, case studies, and ROI projections, and then let them come to their conclusion.

For example,
- "Here's a case study showing how another company reduced downtime by 30%. Feel free to review it and let me know if you have questions. I'm here to help when you're ready."

Provide Transparency and Honesty

Nothing builds trust faster than transparency. When customers feel like they have all the information they need — and no surprises waiting around the corner — they are much more likely to proceed with confidence.

Step 1: Be Honest About Limitations

No product is perfect, and customers appreciate honesty about what your solution can and can't do. If there's an area where your product might fall short, be upfront about it. For instance, "Our platform is ideal for mid-sized companies. While it may not have all the enterprise-level features, we offer scalable add-ons to meet your needs as you grow." This honesty builds trust and shows you have their best interests in mind.

Step 2: Provide Clear Pricing

Customers hate hidden fees and unclear pricing. Be transparent about all costs involved, and ensure they fully understand what they're paying for. When there's no ambiguity, the purchase decision becomes easier, and they're less likely to back out over surprise costs.

Conclusion: Let Customers Buy on Their Terms

Making it easy for customers to buy from you is all about creating an environment where they feel empowered, informed, and in control.

Your job as a salesperson is not to force the sale but to guide them through a process that feels effortless and aligned with their needs.

By simplifying the process, removing friction, being a trusted guide, and offering full transparency, you can transform the buying experience from one of pressure to one of excitement.

Remember, nobody wants to be sold, but everyone loves to buy—so make it easy for them to choose you.

Chapter 12: As a Salesperson – Be on Top of the Process

Success goes beyond just delivering a great pitch. You must manage both the internal
processes within your own organization and the external processes within your customer's company.

Being on top of the entire sales process—from start to finish—ensures deals move efficiently and that no critical details are overlooked.

Salespeople must also play the role of project managers. You'll need to influence internal stakeholders, ensure smooth communication across teams, and manage the customer's buying process without applying too much pressure.

In this chapter, we'll dive into how you can own the entire sales process, manage internal and external factors, and steer deals toward successful closure without alienating anyone.

Why You Must Own the Process

1. Avoiding Delays and Bottlenecks

Sales processes often involve multiple stakeholders and decision-makers. Internally, this could mean navigating through sales, legal, commercial, and technical teams. Externally, you might be dealing with procurement, finance, operations, and executives. Without active management, delays and bottlenecks are inevitable.
By taking ownership of the process, you proactively ensure that each stage moves forward smoothly. If left to chance, deals can stall, approvals can get stuck in limbo, and communication can break down. Owning the process means acting as the project manager who coordinates each step and ensures momentum.

2. Controlling What You Can Control

You might not control every aspect of the process—like how quickly your customer's procurement team approves a contract—but there's still plenty you *can* control. By staying informed and coordinating effectively, you can minimize delays and keep the deal moving forward.

For instance, if you know your legal team takes two weeks to review contracts, submit the paperwork early and set expectations with the customer. If the customer's procurement team needs financials, gather that data upfront to avoid delays when requested.

Your ability to anticipate these needs helps prevent unnecessary bottlenecks.

3. Building Credibility and Trust

Being on top of the process, both internally and externally, builds credibility. It shows that you're not passively waiting for things to happen — you're actively driving the deal forward. This creates trust with your customer, as they see you as someone who's in control and reliable.
On the flip side, if your customer experiences disorganization or sees key details slipping through the cracks, they may question your ability to deliver. Owning the process signals professionalism and competence, reinforcing your value as a partner.

Managing Internal Processes: Coordinating Sales, Commercial, and Technical Teams

1. Understand the Internal Workflow

Every company has its own internal workflow for closing deals. This might involve the sales team handling proposals, the commercial team working out pricing and contracts, the legal team reviewing agreements, and the technical team preparing for implementation. To be on top of the process, you must understand how all these teams work together.

Here's how to manage internal processes effectively:

- **Create a Process Map:** Identify all the steps and key players involved in closing a deal, from the initial pitch to post-sale support. Know how long each step takes, who's responsible for each task, and where potential bottlenecks lie.

- **Set Clear Expectations:** Ensure every internal team knows what's needed from them and by when. For example, make sure the legal team knows when contracts need to be reviewed, and the technical team is ready to deliver once the deal is signed.

- **Anticipate and Prevent Delays:** If certain steps usually cause delays, plan around them. If the legal team historically takes weeks to review contracts, submit them early. If the technical team needs lead time for implementation, communicate that upfront to both your team and the customer.

2. Foster Internal Collaboration

As the salesperson, you're the link between departments. Your job is not just to sell to the customer, but also to ensure internal alignment. Building strong relationships with internal teams is key to making deals happen smoothly.

- **Communicate Often:** Keep everyone in the loop about where the deal stands and what's coming next. Proactive communication prevents surprises and last-minute requests that can cause delays.

- **Be a Facilitator:** Departments often have conflicting priorities. The technical team might need more time for customization, while sales is eager to close. Your job is to mediate these conversations and find compromises.

- **Acknowledge Contributions:** Sales may close the deal, but the entire company plays a role in its success. Recognizing the work of the commercial, legal, or technical teams fosters goodwill and ensures smoother collaboration in the future.

3. Keep the Deal on Track

You're responsible for the deal's success. Once you've coordinated internal stakeholders, ensure nothing falls off the radar. Track deadlines, keep teams accountable, and follow up regularly to maintain momentum.

- **Track Milestones:** Use project management tools or simple spreadsheets to track where the deal stands, what's been completed, and what remains outstanding. Share this timeline with your team so everyone knows their responsibilities.

- **Follow Up Diligently:** When waiting for contract reviews, pricing approvals, or technical specs, follow up regularly to ensure everything stays on track. It's your responsibility to make sure no one drops the ball.

Managing External Processes: Navigating the Customer's Purchasing Process

1. Understand the Customer's Decision-Making Process

Each customer has their own purchasing process. It often involves departments like procurement, finance, legal, and management. Understanding this process is essential to keeping the deal moving.

- **Ask About the Process Early:** Early in discussions, ask the customer to outline their decision-making process. Questions like, "Who needs to approve this?" or "What does your purchasing process look like?" help clarify the path forward.

- **Identify Key Stakeholders:** Know who is involved in the decision beyond your main point of contact. Building relationships with these stakeholders—whether procurement officers or finance directors—ensures you're covering all bases.

2. Influence the Process Without Overstepping

Although you don't have full control over the customer's internal processes, you can still influence them in a positive way. Your job is to guide without overwhelming.

- **Provide All Necessary Information:** Anticipate what the customer will need at each stage, whether it's case studies, pricing details, or technical specs. Proactively providing these materials shows you're a trusted partner and helps keep the process moving.

- **Offer to Help:** Let the customer know you're available to assist with their internal processes. For example, "Would it help if I provided a summary of our ROI analysis for your finance team?"

- **Respect Their Internal Dynamics:** While you may want to speed things up, remember that the customer has their own approval process. Be persistent but respectful—over-pushing can backfire and damage your relationship.

3. Monitor Progress and Keep Communication Open

Just like with your internal teams, you need to track where the deal stands on the customer's side. Regular check-ins with your point of contact help you stay informed of any delays or roadblocks.

- **Set Expectations for Follow-Up:** At the end of each call, clarify when and how you'll follow up. For example, "Can we touch base next week to see how things are progressing?"

- **Stay Engaged Without Being Pushy:** Check in regularly without overwhelming your customer. A simple, "Just checking to see if you need any additional information," keeps the conversation going while respecting their time.

Conclusion: Be the Master of Both Processes

As a salesperson, you're not just closing deals—you're managing processes on both sides.

By owning the internal workflow, fostering collaboration across teams, and navigating the customer's purchasing process without overstepping, you ensure smoother deals and faster closures.

Being on top of the process doesn't mean being pushy. It means staying proactive, helpful, and organized.

When you manage both internal and external factors effectively, you build trust, eliminate bottlenecks, and close deals faster—while ensuring that both your team and your customer see you as a reliable, trusted partner.

Chapter 13:
Customer Is (Not Always) King

—

When to Step Back or Walk Away

As a sales person, we've all heard the famous mantra: "**The customer is king.**" It's a philosophy that emphasizes putting the customer first, bending over backward to meet their needs, and doing everything possible to deliver value.

And while this mindset is crucial to building trust and closing deals, it can sometimes lead to the dangerous belief that you must always say "yes," no matter how outrageous the request.

But here's the truth—you don't need to bow to every demand.

Even kings have limits, and in sales, you've got to know when to hold the line. Not every request is reasonable, not every deal is a winner, and **sometimes the smartest, most profitable move you can make is to step back or walk away entirely.**

Knowing when to set boundaries, protect your business, and make a strategic retreat can be the difference between short-term gain and long-term success.

This chapter is all about mastering that balance—honoring your customer while staying true to your values, your margins, and your strategy. Because at the end of the day, a king without boundaries risks losing his kingdom.

Why the Customer Is Not Always Right

1. Not All Requests Are Realistic

There will be times when a customer asks for the moon—a feature your product doesn't offer, a timeline that's impossible to meet, or a discount so steep it cuts into your profits. Agreeing to these demands can sink your deal faster than a bad pitch. Missed deadlines, overworked teams, and unmet expectations often come from saying "yes" to what should have been a firm "no."

The reality is, saying "no" to an unreasonable demand doesn't mean you're dismissing your customer—it means you're protecting the relationship. When you're upfront about what's possible and what isn't, you set the stage for success instead of failure. You align expectations and create a partnership built on trust and honesty, not overpromising and underdelivering.

2. You Can't Compromise on Values

Every business has its non-negotiables—core values that define who you are and how you operate. If a customer asks you to cut corners, compromise on quality, or engage in practices that go against your principles, it's time to draw a line in the sand.

Remember, compromising your values for a deal today could destroy your credibility tomorrow. A business built on shaky principles will crumble, but one that stands firm on integrity will attract the right customers—those who respect your honesty and ethical standards. Sure, saying "no" might cost you a deal in the short term, but it's the long-term reputation that matters.

Kings may reign, but without integrity, their rule is short-lived.

3. A Bad Deal Can Hurt Your Business

In the rush to close, it's easy to ignore the warning signs of a bad deal. Maybe the customer is asking for discounts that slay your margins, or the scope of the project is way beyond what your team can handle. Pushing through can lead to financial strain, wasted resources, and frustrated teams—all of which damage your reputation.

A bad deal is like a poison pill—it may seem small at first, but over time, it can destroy your business from the inside out. When the costs outweigh the benefits, or when the project stretches your team beyond its limits, walking away is the only move.

Because a **successful business isn't built on winning every deal—it's built on winning the right deals.**

How to Recognize When It's Time to Step Back or Walk Away

1. When the Customer's Demands Are Unreasonable

One of the clearest signs it's time to step back is when the customer's demands start pushing beyond reason. They might be asking for SaaS features far outside your platform's scope, deep discounts that turn profits into pennies, or timelines that would stress even a miracle worker.

How to handle it:

- **Set Clear Boundaries**: Explain why certain requests can't be fulfilled, without closing the door entirely. For instance, "I understand the need for customization, but that's beyond our current capabilities. Here's what we *can* do to help solve your core problem within the platform's limits."

- **Offer Alternatives**: Show that you're committed to solving their problem, even if you can't deliver exactly what they asked for. Offer a solution that meets their needs without compromising your business.

- Know When to Say No: Sometimes, the best thing you can do is politely but firmly say no. It might feel uncomfortable, but it will save you and the customer from unmet expectations and bigger problems down the line.

2. When the Deal Is No Longer Profitable

Profitability is your company's lifeblood. If meeting the customer's demands means cutting so many corners that you're bleeding money or resources, it's time to hit pause. A deal that drains your business isn't a win—it's a loss.

How to evaluate profitability:

- **Calculate the True Cost**: Don't just look at the financials—factor in the time, resources, and effort required. If the deal results in little profit or a loss, reconsider if it's worth pursuing.

- **Weigh Long-Term Impact**: Sometimes a deal that doesn't seem profitable in the short term can be worth it for long-term gains—like breaking into a new market or building a strategic partnership. But if there's no clear long-term benefit, don't chase unprofitable deals.

3. When the Customer Doesn't Align with Your Values

Customers who pressure you to compromise on quality, ethics, or your brand's principles are bad news. They might be offering big money, but the cost to your reputation and team morale isn't worth it. Protect your business and your values by knowing when to walk away.

How to handle value misalignment:

- **Politely Decline**: You don't have to burn bridges. Simply explain, "Our company prioritizes quality, and we wouldn't be able to maintain that if we took shortcuts. Unfortunately, that means we can't move forward under these terms."

- **Stand Firm on Your Principles**: One compromise today can set a precedent for future customers. Protect your integrity, and customers who value ethics and quality will stick around.

4. When the Timing or Relationship Isn't Right

Sometimes, despite your best efforts, the deal just doesn't click. Maybe the timing is off, or the customer's expectations and your capabilities aren't aligned. Forcing a fit where there isn't one won't result in a long-term win. It's better to walk away than to force something that isn't right.

How to assess timing and fit:

- **Evaluate the Fit**: Does the customer's business align with your solution? Are their expectations reasonable? If you keep running into misalignment, the relationship might not be worth pursuing.

- **Assess Timing**: If the customer's priorities or timelines don't match up with yours, it may be better to step back and revisit when the timing aligns better.

How to Walk Away Gracefully

Knowing when to walk away is crucial, but doing it *gracefully* is just as important. It's all about maintaining professionalism and keeping the door open for future opportunities.

1. Be Honest and Transparent

When stepping back, transparency is key. Be upfront and professional about why you're stepping back. For example, "Based on our discussions, it seems like we're not the best fit for what you need right now. We don't want to set unrealistic expectations, so it's best to step back for now."

2. Offer Alternatives

Even if you're walking away, you can still show that you care. Offer alternative solutions that might better fit their needs. This shows that you're invested in their success, even if you're not the one delivering the solution.

3. Leave the Door Open

Walking away doesn't mean slamming the door shut. Circumstances change, and what isn't a fit today might work tomorrow. Leave things on a positive note, letting them know you're open to future conversations when the timing or fit improves.

Conclusion: When the King Must Follow the Rules

While the customer is king, even a king must follow rules. Not every demand is worth fulfilling, not every deal is a good deal, and sometimes the smartest play is to step back or walk away.

By recognizing when it's time to say no, you protect your business, maintain your integrity, and focus your energy on the customers and opportunities that truly matter.

The key is knowing when to walk away and doing it with grace — because walking away is not a sign of defeat; it's a sign of strength, strategy, and long-term vision.

Chapter 14: Make the Deal Happen – Close When the Deal Is Closable

Closing a deal is the ultimate prize. But timing is everything. Push too hard, too soon, and you risk scaring off a customer who's not quite ready. Wait too long, and momentum slips away—leaving room for competitors to swoop in.

The key is knowing when the deal is ripe, seizing that moment, and closing with confidence.

Master closers don't wait for deals to fall into their lap. They understand the delicate balance of guiding customers toward a decision without pressure, all while recognizing the exact moment when it's time to strike.

In this chapter, we'll break down how to read the signals that a deal is ready to close, how to create urgency without being pushy, and how to move confidently to the finish line.

Because when the deal is closable, you need to be ready to make it happen.

Understanding When the Deal Is Ready to Close

1. Look for Buying Signals

Every great closer knows the importance of spotting buying signals—those verbal and non-verbal cues that tell you the customer is ready to pull the trigger. These signals can be subtle, but if you learn to recognize them, you'll know when the time is right.

Common buying signals include:

- **Detailed Questions**: When the customer starts asking specific questions about pricing, contracts, or implementation, it's a clear sign they're thinking seriously about buying.
- **Positive Responses**: If they frequently agree with the value you're offering or emphasize how your solution fits their needs, they're signaling readiness.
- **Involving Key Stakeholders**: Bringing additional decision-makers into the conversation shows the customer is preparing to finalize the deal.

2. Identify the Moment of Peak Interest

Timing is everything. There's often a moment in the sales process when the customer's enthusiasm and interest are at their peak. If you don't close while the excitement is high, you risk losing them to distractions or even competitors.

To spot this moment:

- **Watch for Excitement**: Pay attention when the customer seems genuinely excited about how your solution can solve their problems. This is the prime time to move toward closing.
- **Summarize and Reinforce**: After addressing their pain points and demonstrating value, summarize the key benefits to align with their needs. For example, "It sounds like this solution is exactly what you've been looking for. Are you ready to move forward with the next step?"

3. Ensure All Decision-Makers Are On Board

Before closing, confirm that all the necessary stakeholders are aligned. Deals can stall when a key decision-maker isn't involved or hasn't voiced approval.

Ask direct questions like:
- "Is there anyone else who needs to approve this before we move forward?"
- "Are there any remaining concerns from other stakeholders we need to address?"

Get everyone on the same page before pushing for a close.

Creating a Sense of Urgency Without Pressure

1. Highlight the Consequences of Delay

Sometimes, customers hesitate at the finish line. They need a little push — but not pressure. The best way to create urgency is by highlighting the cost of inaction. What will they lose by waiting?

For example:

- "The longer we wait to implement this solution, the more downtime your team may experience. Moving forward now will allow you to start reducing inefficiencies right away."
- "With our current promotion ending next month, locking in the best rate now ensures you maximize your budget."

Focus on the benefits of acting quickly, without sounding like you're rushing them.

2. Use Timelines and Deadlines

Deadlines can be a powerful motivator. Whether it's a pricing promotion, an upcoming fiscal deadline, or limited product availability, using time-sensitive factors to nudge the customer can create natural urgency.

For instance:

- "Your fiscal year-end is approaching. Implementing this now will allow you to start seeing savings within this year's budget."
- "We're offering a discount for early adopters, but it expires at the end of this quarter."

Deadlines give customers a reason to act without feeling pressured.

3. Frame the Close as the Next Logical Step

Rather than making the close feel like a high-stakes decision, frame it as the natural next step in a process you've both already agreed on.

By now, you've provided the value, answered their questions, and shown how your solution meets their needs. The close should feel like the next obvious move.

For example:

- "It seems like we've covered all the important points, and this solution is a great fit. The next step is to finalize the contract and set up the implementation. Does that work for you?"
- "I think we've addressed everything necessary for you to move forward confidently. Shall we get the paperwork started?"

This approach makes the close feel seamless — like a logical continuation rather than a pressured decision.

Confidently Moving Toward the Close

1. Ask for the Sale

Here's where many salespeople fumble — they hesitate to ask for the sale directly. But your customer expects it. If you've addressed their concerns and built trust, asking for the business isn't pushy — it's professional.

Some effective, non-aggressive closing statements include:

- "It sounds like we're aligned. Shall we go ahead and get this signed today?"
- "Are you ready to move forward with the proposal? I can send the contract right now."
- "I think we're ready to start. Should we finalize the details?"

Confidence is key. If you've built the foundation, asking for the sale should feel like the next step, not a risk.

2. Use the Assumptive Close

The assumptive close is a classic move that works well when the buying signals are strong. Instead of waiting for the customer to say "yes," you lead the conversation as if the deal is already done.

For example:

- "I'll go ahead and schedule the onboarding for next week. Does Tuesday work for you?"
- "Let's set up the kickoff meeting with our implementation team.
  Would you prefer next week or the following?"

This technique makes the decision feel inevitable and smooth, eliminating friction in the process.

3. Handle Last-Minute Objections with Confidence

Even when the deal is closable, customers might throw out last-minute objections. Whether it's concerns about pricing or timing, stay calm and address them head-on.

For example, if they balk at the price:

- "I understand that this is a significant investment. Let's revisit the ROI we discussed. Over the next year, the cost savings and revenue growth will more than cover the upfront cost."

If it's a timing issue:

- "I know you're concerned about timing, but implementing now ensures you can start seeing results before the end of the quarter. We'll work closely with you to make sure everything goes smoothly."

4. Have the Paperwork Ready

When your customer is ready to say "yes," don't let momentum slip. Have everything prepared so they can sign on the dotted line without delay. Whether it's a contract, proposal, or purchase order, be ready to send it over immediately.

For instance:

- "Great! I'll send the contract over now for your signature. Once that's done, we'll move forward."

Being prepared shows professionalism and ensures that you capitalize on the moment.

Conclusion: Sealing the Deal When the Time Is Right

Closing isn't about pressure or manipulation. It's about recognizing when the customer is ready, guiding the process smoothly, and confidently sealing the deal. The art of closing lies in timing, subtle urgency, and creating a natural path forward.

When the deal is closable, don't hesitate—make it happen. Spot the signals, align with decision-makers, and move confidently toward the finish line.

Closing the sale is not just about the transaction; it's about laying the groundwork for a long-term partnership that benefits both you and your customer.

Because when you close the deal at the right moment, you're not just making a sale—you're building trust, delivering value, and securing future success.

Chapter 15: Pitfalls – The Endless Test Installation

One of the most frustrating challenges in sales is when a customer insists on an extended test installation or trial period.

Testing is a crucial step in demonstrating the value of your solution, but when that test turns into an endless cycle, it can drain your resources, stall decision-making, and delay revenue. Customers may prolong the testing phase as a way to avoid making a decision, and that indecision can be costly for you.

Your job as a salesperson is to ensure that while the customer gets the information they need, the trial doesn't become an indefinite drag on your time and resources.

In this chapter, we'll dive into why endless test installations are a trap, how to avoid falling into that trap, and strategies for shortening test periods while keeping the deal on track.

Why Endless Test Installations Hurt Your Sales

1. Resource Drain

Test installations demand resources — time, manpower, technical support — from both your company and the customer. Every day your technical team is setting up, troubleshooting, and adjusting the test, costs are accruing without any guarantee of a deal. This isn't just a financial cost; it's also an opportunity cost. Your team could be focusing on deals that are closer to closing.

The longer the trial, the more it strains your company's resources, reducing your ability to pursue other profitable opportunities.

2. Loss of Momentum

When a test installation drags on, deals lose momentum. Customers can get trapped in a cycle of over-analysis, endlessly testing features and delaying a final decision. The initial excitement that drove the trial fades, and soon, the deal is at risk of going cold. Meanwhile, competitors may swoop in with better offers or faster delivery, potentially taking the deal right out from under you.

3. Delayed Revenue

The longer a test installation continues, the longer you delay generating revenue. Deals that are stuck in an endless testing phase don't contribute to your sales targets, and that delay can have a direct impact on your company's financial health. Until the test concludes and the customer commits, there's no signed contract and no payment.

How to Avoid Endless Test Installations

1. Set Clear Objectives and Success Criteria from the Start

One of the best ways to prevent an endless test installation is by establishing clear objectives and success criteria right from the beginning. Both you and the customer should agree on measurable outcomes that will signal the end of the test and indicate its success.

- **Agree on Measurable Outcomes**: For example, if you're offering a SaaS solution designed to streamline processes, set a specific benchmark like, "We expect to see a 20% reduction in downtime within the first 30 days." Having clear metrics allows you to avoid ambiguity and ensures there's a goal to work toward.

- **Set a Time Limit**: From the start, establish a concrete timeline—30, 60, or 90 days depending on the complexity of the solution. Make it clear that the trial is only for a set period and after that, the next step is to either move forward with the purchase or address any final concerns. For example, "Let's run the test for 60 days. At the end, we'll review the results and make a decision on the next steps."

This creates urgency and a definitive end point, preventing the trial from dragging on.

2. Limit the Scope of the Test

Test installations become endless when the scope gets too broad. The customer may want to try every feature or explore every possible use case, which can easily lead to unnecessary delays. You need to control the scope of the test to focus on the key issues that matter most.

- **Focus on Core Features**: Identify and limit the test to the features that address the customer's biggest challenges. This not only shortens the test time but also makes it easier for the customer to see the value of your solution.

- **Suggest a Phased Approach**: If the customer insists on testing a wide range of features, propose a phased testing approach. Start with the most critical features, and once those are successful, you can expand to secondary features. For example, "Let's focus on the core features first—like the workflow automation. If that works well, we can test additional capabilities later."

3. Set Up Regular Checkpoints

Without regular communication, tests can easily lose focus. Set up structured checkpoints to review progress and keep the trial on track.

- **Weekly or Bi-Weekly Check-Ins**: Schedule check-ins with the customer to review how the test is progressing, address any issues, and ensure the test is meeting the goals you established upfront. For example, "Let's check in every two weeks to ensure we're on track to hit the success metrics we discussed."

- **Adjust the Test if Necessary**: If the test isn't producing the expected results, use these check-ins to troubleshoot and make necessary adjustments. This prevents the customer from extending the trial in hopes of better results later. For example, "It looks like we're not hitting the benchmarks yet. Let's adjust the setup and resolve any issues to keep the test moving forward."

4. Offer a Pilot Agreement Instead of a Free Test

Free test installations often lead to endless trials because there's no financial commitment from the customer. Without money on the line, there's less urgency for them to wrap up the test and make a decision.

A great alternative is offering a **pilot agreement** — a short-term, paid contract that provides a defined test period but with real commitment from the customer.

- **What Is a Pilot Agreement?** It's a paid short-term contract that allows the customer to test the solution under real conditions, but with clear terms regarding duration, scope, and cost. This way, the customer is financially invested, making them more likely to complete the test in a timely manner and move toward a full purchase.

- For example: "We offer a 90-day pilot program at a reduced rate. This allows you to experience the full solution with a set timeline to evaluate results and make a decision."

5. Create a Path to Purchase

From the very beginning, it's important to frame the test installation as a step in the larger buying process, not the final decision-making phase.

- **Discuss the Post-Test Plan Early**: During initial discussions, outline what happens after the test installation. Make it clear that the test is just one phase of the buying process and that the next step is full deployment. For example, "After the test, we'll review the results and move straight into deployment if everything looks good."

- **Prepare the Contract**: As the test period nears completion, have the contract ready to go. By preparing the paperwork ahead of time, you reduce the risk of delays once the test is finished. For example, "Since the test is wrapping up, I'll prepare the contract so we can move forward quickly."

How to Shorten Test Installations

1. Provide Strong Onboarding and Support

A common reason for extended tests is that customers feel they don't fully understand the solution. Make sure the customer's team is fully trained and supported during the test period.

- **Offer Training**: Make sure the customer's team knows how to use the product effectively. The more confident they are, the faster they'll see results and be ready to make a decision.

- **Provide Immediate Support**: Be available to address issues quickly. If a customer's experience is smooth during the test phase, they're more likely to move forward with the purchase.

2. Demonstrate ROI Early

Customers are more likely to shorten the test period when they start seeing positive outcomes early on. Use your check-ins to showcase the benefits the customer is already experiencing, even if the test isn't over yet.

For example: "We've already seen a 15% increase in efficiency during the first two weeks of testing. That's a great sign. Let's keep that momentum going."

Conclusion: Keep the Test Installation on Track

Test installations are a valuable part of the sales process, but they should never drag on indefinitely. By setting clear objectives, limiting the scope, and creating a structured path to purchase, you can prevent the customer from getting stuck in an endless testing loop.

Your job is to keep the process moving—set expectations, provide value early, and guide the customer toward a decision.

When managed effectively, test installations will lead to quicker decisions, stronger relationships, and more closed deals.

Stay in control, and turn every test into a win.

Chapter 16:

Faced with an RFQ You Haven't Influenced? What You Can Do to Win

One of the most daunting challenges in sales is receiving a Request for Quotation (RFQ) or Request for Proposal (RFP) that you had no hand in shaping.

As a salesperson, you want to engage with the customer early, influence the specifications, and ensure the RFQ plays to your strengths.

When you're faced with an RFQ that you haven't influenced, the odds may seem stacked against you — especially if a competitor has already shaped the requirements to favor their solution.

But let me tell you something: **it's not game over**.

Just because you didn't influence the RFQ doesn't mean you can't win. The real test of your skills begins here. How can you approach this situation, differentiate yourself, and turn it to your advantage? That's what we're about to dive into.

Why Not Influencing the RFQ Puts You at a Disadvantage

Typically, salespeople who engage with customers early in the buying process have the inside track. They can shape the RFQ's criteria to favor their offering and, in many cases, subtly exclude competitors.

When you didn't influence the RFQ, you face these disadvantages:

1. Lack of Deep Customer Insight: You may not fully grasp the customer's true needs or underlying motivations. You only see the surface-level specifications, which may not reveal what's really driving their decision.

2. Competitor Influence: If another vendor has already engaged with the customer, the RFQ may be tailored to highlight their strengths and minimize your competitive edge.

3. Late in the Game: The customer may already view your competitors as trusted partners, while you're the latecomer trying to catch up.

Despite these challenges, you can still make a powerful play and turn the situation around.

How to Approach the RFQ You Didn't Influence

1. Analyze the RFQ Thoroughly

Before you dive into crafting your response, you need to deeply analyze the RFQ. What is it really asking for? What's **beneath the surface**?

- **Look for Hidden Needs:** RFQs often focus on technical specs but overlook business goals, operational efficiencies, or future scalability. Ask yourself, "What isn't being said here?" If the RFQ is purely technical, can you uncover underlying business objectives like reducing costs or increasing efficiency? These are areas where you can add value beyond what the RFQ spells out.

- **Spot Competitor Influence**: Pay attention to any specifications that feel unusually specific. If something seems overly tailored, a competitor may have influenced the process. Recognizing this helps you plan your approach: either work around those details or focus on different strengths to break through the competitor's hold.

- **Find Loopholes:** Every RFQ has wiggle room. Look for areas that allow interpretation or flexibility, and think about how you can **differentiate yourself**. Is there room for better support? Faster implementation? Maybe an added service that could set you apart from competitors stuck on technical details.

2. Engage the Customer (If Possible)

Even if you haven't been involved from the start, there's still time to build a relationship. This is where your skills as a closer come into play.

- **Ask Clarifying Questions:** Many RFQs allow vendors to submit clarifications. This is your chance to ask strategic questions that show you're not just interested in checking boxes—you're trying to solve their **real** problems. Ask about their long-term goals, performance metrics, or any specific challenges they face.

- **Offer to Meet:** If the RFQ process permits, reach out for a call or a meeting to discuss their needs in more detail. Even a brief conversation can give you insights into their real pain points. Remember, you're not just competing on price or features—you're building a relationship that your competitors may have neglected.

- **Share Insights:** Go beyond the RFQ. Offer industry insights, case studies, or innovative ideas that weren't explicitly requested but could help the customer make a better decision. This positions you as a trusted advisor, not just a vendor.

3. Differentiate on Value, Not Just Features

When you're responding to an RFQ, it's tempting to stick to technical specs. But remember, **you're not just selling a product—you're selling a solution** that delivers value. That's your differentiator.

- **Focus on ROI:** Even if the RFQ is technical, customers care about results. Demonstrate how your solution will reduce costs, save time, or increase revenue. For instance: "Our solution will cut operational costs by 20%, delivering an estimated savings of $150,000 in the first year alone."

- **Emphasize Long-Term Benefits:** The RFQ might focus on immediate needs, but you should highlight how your solution supports the customer's long-term goals—whether it's scalability, future-proofing, or reduced maintenance. Customers want solutions that last.

- **Provide a Total Solution:** Beyond features, what else can you offer? Can you bundle training, ongoing support, or consulting services to enhance the customer's experience? Show that you're not just a vendor; you're a partner invested in their success.

4. Offer Alternatives or Added Value

You may feel locked into the RFQ's requirements, but that doesn't mean you can't offer more.

- **Suggest Value-Added Features:** Even if the RFQ doesn't explicitly ask for it, consider offering training, extended warranties, or premium support. It shows that you're going the extra mile. For instance: "In addition to meeting the RFQ specs, we offer hands-on training to ensure your team gets up to speed quickly."

- **Propose Alternatives:** Sometimes, the RFQ's requirements are too narrow. Don't be afraid to suggest an alternative solution that delivers better results. Present it as a value proposition: "While we meet your technical requirements, we believe our alternative approach could save you 20% on long-term costs."

5. Leverage Your Differentiators

Even without influencing the RFQ, you have **unique strengths** that your competitors can't match.

- **Industry Expertise:** If you have deep experience in their industry, emphasize it. Case studies and testimonials from similar customers can make a strong case. "With 15 years of experience in your industry, we've helped companies like yours increase efficiency by 30%."

- **Customer Support:** Many RFQs overlook the importance of customer support. Highlight how your support model goes beyond the industry standard. For example: "We offer 24/7 dedicated support, ensuring minimal downtime and fast issue resolution."

- **Innovation:** If your solution includes innovative features, such as AI or advanced analytics, highlight how it can give the customer a competitive edge. "Our AI-powered analytics provide real-time insights, helping you make faster decisions and improve efficiency by 25%."

6. Price Strategically

When you haven't influenced the RFQ, pricing becomes critical.
But remember, **it's not just about being the lowest bidder.**

- **Justify Your Price with Value:** If your price is higher, explain why. Show the customer how your solution's total cost of ownership (TCO) saves money over time, reduces risk, or provides better results. "While our price is higher upfront, the TCO is lower due to fewer maintenance requirements, saving you 30% over five years."

- **Offer Flexible Pricing**: If the customer is price-sensitive, consider offering tiered pricing or flexible payment options. Give them choices that align with their budget and still deliver value.

- **Emphasize TCO**: When price is the main concern, focus on the TCO, not just the initial cost. Show how your solution will save money long-term through efficiency gains, reduced maintenance, or lower operational costs.

Conclusion: Winning the RFQ You Didn't Influence

Facing an RFQ you didn't influence can feel like you're behind the eight ball, but don't throw in the towel. **This is where real closers shine.**

By analyzing the RFQ, engaging the customer, and focusing on value, you can position yourself to win—even if the odds seem stacked against you.

Start by identifying hidden needs, engaging with the customer to clarify objectives, and emphasizing what sets you apart. Bring the conversation back to **value and results**, not just technical specs. Finally, price strategically and highlight your differentiators.

Even if you weren't part of the RFQ's creation, with the right approach, you can turn a tough situation into a winning opportunity. **This is where top salespeople thrive**—not just in perfect conditions, but in the face of adversity.

Go get it.

Chapter 17:

Talk on Eye Level: You Are the Doctor to Ease Your Customer's Pain

In sales, there's a misconception that the only way to close a deal is to "win over" the customer.

This often leads to salespeople feeling inferior or desperate to gain the customer's attention, especially when dealing with high-level executives or large corporations. But this mindset leads to self-doubt, weak communication, and a loss of control over the conversation.

Here's the truth: you are not inferior to your customer.

In fact, you are their equal—an expert and a professional there to solve problems. Imagine yourself as a doctor, coming in with the skills to diagnose your customer's pain points and prescribe the perfect solution.

Approach your sales conversations on equal footing, with confidence and authority, and you'll shift the dynamic in your favor, creating mutual respect and better outcomes for everyone involved.

In this chapter, we'll explore why sales conversations should be collaborations between equals, how to position yourself as a trusted advisor, and how to use your expertise to bring real relief to your customer's pain.

Why You Are Not Inferior to Your Customer

1. You Bring Valuable Expertise

You're not in that room just to "sell" — you're there because you bring expertise. While your customer knows their business, **you know your solution, the market, and industry best practices**. That makes you an asset.

Customers reach out because they can't solve these problems alone — they need a professional, and that's where you come in.

Just like a doctor, your role is to ask the right questions, understand the pain, and offer a solution that improves their situation.

2. You're Providing Solutions, Not Selling Products

Your value doesn't come from what you're selling but from **how well you solve the customer's unique challenges**. This mindset shift is critical. If you view yourself as just another salesperson, you'll constantly feel under pressure. But when you understand that your role is to solve rather than to sell, you're no longer pushing products — you're empowering the customer to overcome obstacles, achieve their goals, and grow their business. This puts you on equal footing, positioning you as a vital partner in their success.

3. Mutual Respect Drives Success

Healthy sales relationships are built on **mutual respect**. When you approach a sales conversation on eye level, the customer respects you for the value you bring, and you respect the customer for their openness and willingness to engage. If you go in feeling inferior, you'll lose this balance, overcompensating by offering discounts or bending over backward to please.

But when you see yourself as equal, the conversation centers on what matters — solving problems, building trust, and achieving results.

How to Approach Sales Conversations as Equals

1. Understand Your Role as a Doctor of Solutions

Think of your role like a doctor's. Customers come to you because they have pain — whether it's operational inefficiencies, stagnant growth, or high costs. Your job is to **listen, diagnose, and prescribe a solution** that relieves that pain.

Step 1: Diagnose the Problem

Start by identifying the customer's pain points with insightful, open-ended questions that encourage them to share details:

- "What challenges are you currently facing in your operations?"
- "Where do you see inefficiencies impacting your bottom line?"
- "What's keeping you from reaching your growth targets?"

Step 2: Prescribe the Solution

Once you've uncovered the problem, **prescribe a solution that meets their needs**. Instead of pushing a generic pitch, offer a targeted solution as the remedy for their pain.

- "Based on what you've shared, our solution can reduce your operational downtime by 20%, which translates to a 15% productivity boost. Let's discuss how we can make that happen quickly."

2. Project Confidence and Authority

Confidence is everything in sales. When you believe in your solution and the value you bring, that confidence naturally comes through in your voice, body language, and approach. Customers will trust and respect you more when you project this authority.

Step 1: Own Your Expertise

You know your product, the market, and the competition inside and out—lean on that expertise. Show the customer that you're not just here to sell but to advise.

- "In my experience working with similar companies, we've seen these kinds of inefficiencies significantly reduced with the right tools in place. Let's talk about how we can achieve the same for you."

Step 2: Use Assertive, Not Aggressive, Language

Confidence doesn't mean being pushy. It means being assertive, clear, and direct about the value you're offering. Avoid apologetic language like "I'm just hoping this could help" and instead use statements like "I believe this solution directly addresses your challenges."

- Instead of saying: "I think this might help with your problem." Say: "I'm confident this solution will solve the challenges you've been experiencing."

3. Engage on Eye Level: It's a Partnership

Treat your customer as an equal in the conversation, not as someone you're trying to win over. This interaction should be a partnership where both sides contribute and benefit.

Step 1: Ask for Their Input and Expertise

Just as you bring your industry expertise, the customer brings their business insights. **Respect their knowledge** by asking questions that show you value their input. This strengthens the relationship and ensures your solution is tailored to their specific needs.

- "You know your business better than anyone. Where do you see the biggest challenges, and how can we work together to address them?"

Step 2: Position the Conversation as a Collaboration

Frame the sales process as a joint effort to find the best solution. When you do this, you're no longer "selling" but collaborating. The customer sees you as a trusted partner, not a salesperson looking for a quick close.

- "Let's work together to ensure we're addressing your top priorities. My goal is to help you implement a solution that drives real results."

4. Recognize When to Walk Away

An equal partnership means recognizing when the fit isn't right. Sometimes, the customer's needs don't align with your solution, or their expectations are unrealistic. Walking away is a sign of confidence. It shows that you're not desperate for every deal—you're focused on customers who genuinely benefit from your solution.

- "Based on what we've discussed, it seems our solution might not be the best fit for your current needs. Let's keep the door open in case your priorities shift."

How to Shift Your Mindset Toward Equality

1. Recognize Your Value

You are the bridge between the customer's problem and the solution. Without you, they might not even realize their challenges or missed opportunities. Start seeing yourself as a solution provider—not a seller.

2. Focus on the Customer's Outcomes

Shifting your mindset from "I need to close this deal" to "I need to help this customer succeed" reframes the entire conversation. Now, you're not just aiming for a sale—you're working together to solve problems and achieve success.

3. Prepare Thoroughly

Confidence is built on preparation. The more you understand the customer's business, industry, and pain points, the more confidently you can engage on eye level. Do your homework so that you're fully prepared for every meeting.

Conclusion: You Are the Doctor to Ease Your Customer's Pain

Sales isn't about begging for deals—it's about **solving problems.** When you approach every conversation with the confidence of a doctor diagnosing a patient, you're not chasing the customer for approval. Instead, you're building a partnership where both sides bring expertise to the table.

Remember, you are not inferior to your customer. **You're here to provide value, ease their pain, and help them succeed**. Approach every conversation with this mindset, and you'll project confidence, foster mutual respect, and, ultimately, close more deals.

Chapter 18:
Tools Make Your Life Easier

Winning isn't just about the product or a polished pitch - it's about working smarter.

Sales tools have become indispensable, giving sales professionals the power to streamline processes, uncover valuable insights, and make fast, informed decisions.

With the right tools, you can skip the busywork, bypass gatekeepers, and connect with the people who matter most, getting you closer to closing deals.

From LinkedIn for networking to Seamless.ai for direct contacts and The Official Board for insights into company structures, the right tools can boost your success in today's fast-paced sales environment.

This chapter focuses on essential tools that simplify your workflow, enhance your understanding of target customers, and make it easier to reach key contacts.

Why Tools Are Essential in Modern Sales

1. Time Efficiency: Less Searching, More Selling

In sales, time is everything. The less time you spend searching for contacts or gathering data, the more time you have to build relationships and close deals. Sales tools help you skip the legwork and get straight to selling by providing quick access to contacts, direct information, and company insights.

2. Deeper Customer Insights

Today's customers expect you to know them before they know you. Sales tools offer in-depth insights into potential customers, their organizational structure, and even their pain points. With this knowledge, you can tailor your approach in a way that resonates with decision-makers and improves your chances of success.

3. Bypassing Gatekeepers

Gatekeepers are a common hurdle in sales — receptionists, assistants, and middle managers who filter calls and emails before they reach decision-makers. With the right tools, you can skip the gatekeepers altogether and go directly to the people who matter, whether through direct email or phone contacts.

Tools That Make Your Life Easier

1. LinkedIn: The Networking Powerhouse

LinkedIn isn't just for building a professional profile; it's a goldmine for prospecting, networking, and understanding your target customers. With its 900 million members, LinkedIn gives you access to decision-makers across industries worldwide.

How to Use LinkedIn Effectively

Research Your Audience: Use LinkedIn's search features to find decision-makers based on criteria like job title, company, industry, or location. If you're focused on manufacturing, for example, search for executives or procurement managers in that space.

Understand Organizational Structure: LinkedIn's connections allow you to see reporting relationships within a company, helping you identify stakeholders and their influence.

Engage Before Outreach: Start by engaging with your prospects—comment on their posts, share relevant articles, or send a connection request with a thoughtful note.

Example:
- "Hi [Prospect's Name], I read your post on [topic] and work with companies like [their company] to tackle similar challenges. I'd love to connect and exchange insights."

Use LinkedIn Sales Navigator: For more advanced targeting, Sales Navigator offers deeper filters, prospect alerts, and recommendations for ideal contacts.

2. Seamless.ai: Find Direct Contacts Instantly

Seamless.ai helps you find accurate contact information, including direct phone numbers and email addresses for the decision-makers you're targeting. This tool is a time-saver, delivering the data you need to get to the right person without the usual hurdles.

How to Use Seamless.ai

Search by Company or Title: Seamless.ai allows you to input a company or title and retrieve direct contact details instantly.

LinkedIn Integration: Seamless.ai integrates with LinkedIn, so while you browse profiles, you can access direct contact details without leaving LinkedIn.

Bypass Gatekeepers: Direct email and phone contact lets you skip the main switchboard and reach out confidently.

Example:
- "Hi [Prospect's Name], I work with companies like [their company] to improve operations. Could we set up a quick call to explore some ideas?"

3. The Official Board: Understand Organizational Structures

The Official Board provides comprehensive organizational charts, showing key decision-makers and their reporting lines within companies worldwide. This tool is especially valuable when you need to understand who influences purchasing decisions and the roles of different stakeholders.

How to Use The Official Board

Identify Decision-Makers: View the company's hierarchy to see which executives hold decision-making power and who influences them.

Understand Relationships: Knowing the reporting structure helps you plan outreach effectively — if a CFO reports directly to the CEO, for example, you can tailor your pitch to align with both roles' goals.

Leverage Connections: Use mutual connections for warm introductions or referrals. If a colleague knows a target executive, a referral can increase your chances of a response.

4. Hunter.io: Find Verified Email Addresses

Hunter.io is excellent for finding and verifying email addresses linked to a specific domain, which is useful when you know the company but need an individual's contact details. This tool helps ensure you're contacting the right person.

How to Use Hunter.io

Domain Search: Search by domain (e.g., companyname.com) to find standard email formats used within a company.

Email Verification: Hunter.io also verifies emails, reducing the risk of bounces and ensuring your emails reach their targets.

5. Crystal Knows: Personalize Communication

Crystal Knows uses AI to analyze a prospect's personality based on LinkedIn and other online data, helping you adapt your communication style to theirs. Whether they prefer direct language, casual tone, or detailed info, Crystal Knows optimizes your outreach style.

How to Use Crystal Knows

Tailor Your Messaging: Crystal Knows provides personality profiles, helping you understand whether your prospect is analytical, results-driven, or action-oriented. This allows you to match their preferred tone and style.

Enhance Email and Call Effectiveness: Aligning your messaging with their preferences increases the likelihood of a positive response.

Example:

- For an executive who values efficiency, "I'll keep this brief: Our solution could reduce your costs by 15% within six months. Let's discuss this further."

Putting It All Together: Streamlining Sales with Tools

Using these tools in tandem can help you optimize the sales process, improve outreach quality, and connect with decision-makers more effectively.

1. **Start with LinkedIn**: Use LinkedIn to research your target company, identify key decision-makers, and build rapport through engagement.
2. **Find Contact Information with Seamless.ai or Hunter.io**: Once you have the right contacts, use Seamless.ai or Hunter.io to secure email addresses or phone numbers.
3. **Understand Company Hierarchy with The Official Board**: Use The Official Board to get a clear picture of the company structure and tailor your approach to specific influencers.
4. **Personalize Outreach with Crystal Knows**: Use Crystal Knows to match your communication style with the prospect's personality.
5. **Follow Up Consistently**: Use these tools to maintain a consistent follow-up strategy. A well-timed message can be the difference between closing a deal or being ignored.

Conclusion: Tools Empower Smarter Selling

Today's sales professionals have access to a wealth of tools that make prospecting, outreach, and relationship-building more efficient than ever. From using Seamless.ai to bypass gatekeepers, to gaining organizational insights with The Official Board, and personalizing your approach with Crystal Knows, these tools empower you to work smarter and get results faster.

The key is to integrate these kind of tools into your daily workflow and make them part of a strategic approach to sales. With the right tools at your disposal, you can streamline your processes, reach key decision-makers, and close more deals confidently.

Disclaimer:
I´m in no relation with the producers, vendors or sellers of the here given examples and tool names. I´m not selling those or get paid for mentioning these examples. There are multiple options for similar tool chains – please compare and find those who fit best for you!

Chapter 18: You Don't Always Need to Tell the Bad Things if You're Not Asked!

Sales is built on trust, and customers expect honesty from salespeople. The quickest way to damage your reputation and lose a deal is by misleading a prospect.

But honesty doesn't mean offering every potential drawback or limitation of your product upfront. Effective communication is about focusing on the value you bring and only addressing concerns when they arise.

In this chapter, we'll explore the balance between transparency and over-disclosure. You should always be truthful, but you don't need to bring up negative information unless it directly impacts the customer's needs or concerns.

The goal is to highlight the value of your solution, handle objections professionally when they come up, and maintain integrity throughout the sales process.

Why Lying Damages Trust and Kills Deals

1. Customers Always Find Out

In today's world, customers have endless access to reviews, insights, and resources. Misleading prospects about your product's capabilities or hiding key details only leads to disappointment when the truth comes out. Once a customer feels misled, it's nearly impossible to regain their trust — and you risk not just losing the deal but also your reputation.

2. Broken Trust Means Lost Relationships

Closing a deal through dishonest tactics can lead to an unstable relationship. When customers discover that you haven't been fully honest, they're unlikely to do business with you again, and they'll share their negative experience with others. Trust is foundational to future opportunities and long-term success.

Why You Don't Need to Offer Negative Information Unless Asked

1. Focus on What Matters to the Customer

Honesty is essential, but you don't need to proactively share every potential drawback if it isn't directly relevant to the customer's goals. Every product has limitations, but if these don't affect the customer's main concerns, there's no need to emphasize them. Instead, focus on how your solution addresses their pain points and brings them closer to their goals.

For instance, if a customer is mainly interested in improving operational efficiency, they likely don't need to hear about features your product lacks. Raising these could introduce unnecessary doubts, even if they're irrelevant to their priorities.

2. Every Product Has Trade-offs

No product is flawless. Each solution comes with trade-offs, whether in price, features, or support options. Customers are often willing to accept minor downsides if the overall value of your solution outweighs them. By focusing on strengths, you keep the conversation productive. If a limitation matters to the customer and they ask about it, answer honestly, but don't volunteer every potential downside that may not impact their decision.

3. You're Selling Solutions, Not Perfection

Your job isn't to sell a flawless product—it's to provide a solution that addresses the customer's problems. Even if your product has minor shortcomings, if it fulfills their needs and adds value, those limitations become secondary. For example, if your software is missing a competitor's feature but excels in usability and scalability—qualities that the customer values—focus on those strengths. Don't bring up irrelevant issues unless specifically asked.

How to Handle Objections with Honesty

1. Address Questions Honestly but Strategically

When customers raise objections or ask about a possible drawback, answer truthfully but frame your response to keep the focus on the value you bring. If a customer inquires about a missing feature, acknowledge it and redirect to the benefits your solution offers.

Example:

- **Customer**: "Does your solution have X feature?"
- **You**: "We don't offer that feature at the moment, but our approach is highly streamlined, which means faster deployment and easier usability. Many of our customers prefer this simplicity as it saves them time and resources."

By acknowledging the limitation while highlighting the positives, you handle the objection with integrity and keep the conversation productive.

2. Pivot to the Bigger Picture

If a customer asks about a specific limitation, use the opportunity to shift back to the broader value your solution provides. This keeps the focus on the benefits and helps the customer put the limitation into perspective.

Example:

- **Customer**: "Do you offer 24/7 support like your competitor?"
- **You**: "We don't have 24/7 support, but our dedicated account managers and fast response times during business hours consistently earn us high customer satisfaction. Our customers find that they get more personalized, effective support."

This reframes the conversation, showing that what you offer may better suit their needs overall.

3. Turn a Weakness into a Strength

Sometimes, what might seem like a limitation can be reframed as an advantage, depending on the customer's priorities. If your product is simpler than a competitor's, this can be a benefit for customers who want user-friendliness and less complexity.

Example:

- **Customer**: "Your solution has fewer features than the competitor."
- **You**: "Yes, and we designed it that way on purpose. Our customers value simplicity, which allows them to implement and maintain it more easily and see faster ROI without unnecessary features."

Reframing helps the customer focus on how these strengths address their needs.

Knowing When Full Transparency Is Necessary

1. When the Limitation Could Affect Their Success

If a limitation in your product could significantly impact the customer's success, it's crucial to mention it upfront. This proactive approach prevents future frustration and maintains trust.

Example:

- "I want to be honest with you—our solution doesn't currently integrate with that system. However, we've worked with other clients in similar situations and found effective workarounds. I'd be happy to discuss these options with your team."

2. When the Customer's Expectations Are Misaligned

If a customer's expectations don't match what your product delivers, you need to clarify to avoid disappointment later. Being upfront might mean the customer isn't the right fit, but honesty builds credibility and keeps the door open for future opportunities.

Example:

- "It sounds like you're looking for a highly customizable solution. Our platform focuses more on ease of use and quick deployment, so it might not be the best fit for your current needs. I'd rather make sure we're a good match before moving forward."

Conclusion: Honesty Without Over-Disclosure

In sales, honesty is essential. But honesty doesn't mean volunteering every minor flaw or limitation of your product, especially when those issues don't impact the customer's needs.

Your role is to guide them toward a solution, focusing on the value you bring while addressing only the relevant concerns as they come up.

By balancing transparency and strategic communication, you can maintain trust, effectively handle objections, and close deals without undermining your credibility. Remember, you're not selling perfection—you're delivering solutions.

Focus on how your product meets the customer's needs, and only discuss potential negatives when they're directly relevant.

Chapter 19: Forget BANT. For Complex Sales Situations, MEDPICC Is a Better Method

In Sales situations many of us have relied on the BANT framework—Budget, Authority, Need, and Timing - to qualify leads.

BANT works well for straightforward, fast-cycle sales, where decision-making is relatively simple. It helps identify whether a prospect has the budget to afford your solution, the authority to make the decision, a clear need, and the right timing for a purchase.

However, in complex sales situations—especially those with multiple stakeholders, long sales cycles, and high-dollar deals—BANT often falls short.

In these scenarios, you need something more robust, and that's where **MEDPICC** comes in.

In this chapter, we'll dive into why BANT may miss the mark in complex sales and how **MEDPICC** (Metrics, Economic Buyer, Decision Criteria, Decision Process, Paper Process, Identify Pain, Champion, and Competition) provides a more comprehensive framework.

We'll also explore how to apply MEDPICC to better understand your customer's buying process and increase your odds of closing high-stakes deals.

Why BANT Can Fall Short in Complex Sales

1. BANT Oversimplifies the Buying Process

While BANT is helpful for understanding basic customer qualifications, it's often too simplistic for complex sales.

Complex deals involve many decision-makers, departments, and approval processes. In these cases, simply knowing that someone has the budget and the authority isn't enough — you need a deep understanding of the decision-making process, including the internal dynamics and politics.

For instance, in a large enterprise sale, you might identify a mid-level manager who has some authority and budget, but they're only one voice in a broader committee. Without a full view of the process, you could find yourself stuck in endless discussions, unable to push the deal forward.

2. Complex Sales Involve More Than Just Need

While BANT focuses heavily on identifying the need, complex sales often involve multiple needs and conflicting priorities across departments. In a lengthy sales cycle, what starts as a single need often expands into multiple pain points and objectives. BANT might help you spot the initial need, but it doesn't always reveal how this need fits into the organization's strategic goals.

3. Timing Alone Isn't Enough

Timing is crucial, but in complex deals, sales cycles are rarely linear. Numerous approval stages, shifting priorities, and unforeseen delays mean timing can change repeatedly. BANT assumes that if timing is right, the deal will progress smoothly.

In reality, understanding the **Decision Process** and **Paper Process** — the chain of approvals and contract steps — is key to driving complex deals to closure.

Introducing MEDPICC: The Framework for Complex Sales

In more intricate sales scenarios, MEDPICC offers a robust framework to navigate all the moving parts of a complex sale. Each letter represents a critical aspect of the buying process you need to understand and manage to close high-value deals.

Here's what MEDPICC stands for:

- **Metrics:** The quantifiable outcomes the customer wants to achieve.
- **Economic Buyer:** The individual with the ultimate financial authority.
- **Decision Criteria:** The specific standards the customer uses to evaluate solutions.
- **Decision Process:** The steps the customer will take to make the final decision.
- **Paper Process:** The formal steps required to finalize contracts and approvals.
- **Identify Pain:** The core pain points driving the customer to seek a solution.
- **Champion:** Your internal advocate who's pushing for your solution.
- **Competition:** The other vendors or solutions your prospect is considering.

Breaking Down MEDPICC

1. Metrics – Quantify the Value of Your Solution

Metrics are the measurable outcomes your customer seeks with your solution. In complex sales, it's crucial to define what success looks like for your customer in tangible terms. This could be reducing operational costs, improving efficiency, or increasing revenue. By pinpointing these metrics, you directly tie your solution to the customer's desired outcomes, making ROI evident.

Key Questions:

- What metrics does the customer use to measure success?
- How will they quantify the value of your solution?

Example:

- "Our solution will reduce production downtime by 20%, translating to an annual savings of $500,000."

2. Economic Buyer – Identify the Person with Financial Authority

The Economic Buyer has the ultimate say in approving the purchase. Often, this person is more concerned with financial impact than technical details. Knowing who this person is and understanding their priorities can be pivotal in complex sales.

Key Questions:

- Who holds final budget approval?
- What financial outcomes matter most to them?

Example:

- "The VP of Operations is the decision-maker for large investments, primarily concerned with reducing operational costs."

3. Decision Criteria – Understand How Decisions Are Made

Every organization has Decision Criteria – the standards they use to evaluate solutions. These could include factors like price, scalability, ease of implementation, or customer support. Knowing these criteria helps you tailor your pitch to meet the customer's priorities.

Key Questions:

- What criteria will the customer use to evaluate solutions?
- Are they focused more on cost, scalability, or support?

Example:

- "The customer's key criteria are integration with existing systems and robust post-implementation support."

4. Decision Process – Map Out the Buying Journey

The Decision Process includes all the steps the customer must take to reach a final decision, from internal approvals to external consulting. Complex sales often involve numerous departments and decision-makers, so mapping this process keeps you in control of the timeline.

Key Questions:

- What steps need to happen to close the deal?
- Who else is involved in the approval process?

Example:

- "The deal requires legal and procurement approval before going to the CFO for final sign-off."

5. Paper Process – Navigate the Contracting Process

In complex sales, the Paper Process involves legal reviews, contract negotiations, and compliance checks. Understanding this process helps prevent last-minute delays.

Key Questions:

- What steps are needed to finalize the contract?
- How long does the approval process usually take?

Example:

- "The legal team typically requires 3-4 weeks to review contracts, followed by a procurement check."

6. Identify Pain – Pinpoint the Customer's Pain Points

Identifying the customer's core Pain is essential because it reveals what's driving them to seek a solution. In complex sales, these pain points are often layered, involving operational inefficiencies, strategic goals, or regulatory concerns.

Key Questions:

- What challenges or pain points is the customer addressing?
- How does this pain impact their business?

Example:
- "The customer faces high maintenance costs and downtime, causing delays in shipments and revenue loss."

7. Champion – Leverage an Internal Advocate

Your Champion is your advocate within the customer's organization who believes in your solution. A strong champion can be the difference in complex sales, helping you navigate internal politics and keep your solution top of mind.

Key Questions:

- Who is advocating for your solution within the organization?
- How influential are they with other decision-makers?

Example:

- "The head of IT is a strong supporter and has been pushing for our solution in their infrastructure overhaul."

8. Competition – Understand the Competitive Landscape

Competition represents the other options the customer is considering. Understanding who your competitors are and how they're positioning themselves is crucial in setting yourself apart. Be aware of the incumbent vendor or any vendor the customer has a prior relationship with.

Key Questions:

- Who else is the customer considering?
- How does the customer perceive your competitors?

Example:

- "The customer is considering a lower-cost competitor but has concerns about their support and implementation capabilities."

Conclusion: When Complexity Demands More Than BANT

While BANT remains useful for simpler, transactional sales, MEDPICC offers a comprehensive framework for high-stakes deals. Complex sales demand a deep understanding of your customer's internal dynamics, their decision-making processes, and the root of their pain points.

Using MEDPICC, you can methodically approach each critical aspect of the sale, helping you anticipate needs, build trust, and position yourself as the preferred solution.

Taking the time to apply MEDPICC uncovers the details needed to tailor your approach, build rapport with decision-makers, and significantly boost your chances of winning complex sales.

Sources for "Hugging the Gorilla – or my little incomplete Sales Book"

Creating a comprehensive guide on modern sales strategies involves synthesizing a wide range of knowledge, frameworks, and best practices developed by industry experts over the years.

The chapters in this book draw upon well-established sales methodologies, contemporary theories, and practical insights from successful sales professionals.
Below is a list of key sources and references that influenced the content of each chapter:

General Sales Frameworks and Methodologies

1. **BANT (Budget, Authority, Need, Timing)**
    - **Source:** Developed by IBM in the 1960s.
    - **Description:** A framework to assess the viability of prospects based on their budget, authority to make decisions, need for the product or service, and timing of their purchase.

2. **MEDPICC (Metrics, Economic Buyer, Decision Criteria, Decision Process, Paper Process, Identify Pain, Champion, Competition)**
   - **Source:** Based on the MEDDIC sales qualification framework, originally developed by Jack Napoli and popularized by Jack Daly.
   - **Description:** An extended version of MEDDIC, tailored for complex sales environments, emphasizing comprehensive qualification criteria to navigate intricate buying processes and close high-value deals.

3. **Sandler Training Methodology**
   - **Source:** Founded by David Sandler in 1967.
   - **Description:** A sales training program emphasizing relationship-building, qualifying leads, and sales control through communication techniques, designed to drive sales success with a consultative, question-driven approach.

4. **Sales Funnel vs. Sales Pipeline**
   - **Source:** Common sales terminology and practices in sales management literature.
   - **Description:** Differentiates between the customer-centric journey of the sales funnel and the salesperson-centric management tool of the sales pipeline.

Books and Publications

5. **"SPIN Selling" by Neil Rackham**
   - **Influence:** Techniques for effective questioning and understanding customer needs.

- **Key Concepts:** Situation, Problem, Implication, Need-Payoff questions.

6. **"The Challenger Sale" by Matthew Dixon and Brent Adamson**
   - **Influence:** Emphasis on teaching, tailoring, and taking control in sales interactions.
   - **Key Concepts:** Challenging customer assumptions and providing unique insights.

7. **"Solution Selling" by Michael Bosworth**
   - **Influence:** Focus on selling solutions rather than products.
   - **Key Concepts:** Identifying customer pain points and aligning solutions to address them.

8. **"New Sales. Simplified." by Mike Weinberg**
   - **Influence:** Strategies for new business development and sales pipeline management.
   - **Key Concepts:** Effective prospecting, pipeline building, and sales presentation techniques.

9. **"The Sales Development Playbook" by Trish Bertuzzi**
   - **Influence:** Modern sales development strategies and tools.
   - **Key Concepts:** Lead generation, outbound sales tactics, and leveraging technology in sales.

Online Resources and Articles

10. **HubSpot Sales Blog**
    - **Influence:** Practical tips, strategies, and updates on sales best practices.

- **Key Concepts:** Sales pipeline management, lead nurturing, and sales technology.

11. **Salesforce Resources**
    - **Influence:** Comprehensive guides and whitepapers on CRM, pipeline management, and sales forecasting.
    - **Key Concepts:** Leveraging CRM tools for effective pipeline management and sales analytics.

12. **LinkedIn Sales Solutions**
    - **Influence:** Insights on leveraging LinkedIn for sales prospecting and relationship building.
    - **Key Concepts:** Social selling, using LinkedIn Sales Navigator, and building a professional network.

Sales Tools and Technologies

13. **LinkedIn Sales Navigator**
    - **Influence:** Best practices for using LinkedIn as a sales prospecting tool.
    - **Key Concepts:** Advanced search filters, lead recommendations, and relationship management.

14. **Seamless.ai**
    - **Influence:** Strategies for finding direct contact information and bypassing gatekeepers.

- **Key Concepts:** Automated lead generation, data accuracy, and integration with CRM systems.

15. **The Official Board**
    - **Influence:** Techniques for understanding organizational structures and identifying key decision-makers.
    - **Key Concepts:** Organizational charts, stakeholder mapping, and strategic outreach.

16. **Hunter.io**
    - **Influence:** Methods for finding and verifying email addresses for sales outreach.
    - **Key Concepts:** Email verification, domain search, and compliance with email outreach best practices.

17. **Crystal Knows**
    - **Influence:** Personalizing communication based on personality insights.
    - **Key Concepts:** Tailoring sales messages, understanding communication styles, and enhancing engagement.

Sales Training and Thought Leadership

18. **RAIN Group**
    - **Influence:** Research-based sales strategies and performance improvement.
    - **Key Concepts:** Solution selling, consultative selling, and sales effectiveness.

19. **Sales Hacker**
    - **Influence:** Community-driven insights, webinars, and articles on advanced sales techniques.
    - **Key Concepts:** Modern sales tactics, technology in sales, and sales leadership.

Academic and Industry Research

20. **Harvard Business Review (HBR)**
    - **Influence:** Research articles and case studies on sales strategy and management.
    - **Key Concepts:** Sales innovation, customer relationship management, and strategic selling.
21. **Gartner and Forrester Reports**
    - **Influence:** Industry research and analysis on sales trends and technologies.
    - **Key Concepts:** Sales technology adoption, buyer behavior, and market dynamics.

Personal Experiences and Case Studies

22. **Interviews with Sales Professionals**
    - **Influence:** Real-world insights and anecdotes from experienced salespeople.
    - **Key Concepts:** Practical applications of sales frameworks, overcoming challenges, and success stories.

23. **Case Studies from Successful Companies**
    - **Influence:** Examples of effective sales strategies and pipeline management in various industries.
    - **Key Concepts:** Best practices, lessons learned, and replicable strategies.

Conclusion

The content of "*Hugging the Gorilla – or - My Little Incomplete Sales Book*" is built on recognized sales frameworks, expert insights from leading sales literature, and practical strategies from industry resources. By integrating these sources, the book provides a well-rounded, actionable guide for modern sales professionals in today's complex B2B market.

For further reading, the following books and resources are highly recommended:

- "SPIN Selling" by Neil Rackham
- "The Challenger Sale" by Matthew Dixon and Brent Adamson
- "Solution Selling" by Michael Bosworth
- "New Sales. Simplified." by Mike Weinberg
- "The Sales Development Playbook" by Trish Bertuzzi
- Sandler Training Programs and Resources
- MEDPICC Resources
- HubSpot Sales Blog
- Salesforce Resources
- LinkedIn Sales Solutions Blog
- Sales Hacker
- Harvard Business Review (Sales Section)
- Gartner and Forrester Sales Reports

Using these resources, you can expand your knowledge, refine your strategies, and enhance your effectiveness as a trusted advisor to customers.

Why should you buy "Hugging the Gorilla"?

Because in sales, it's not about knowing *everything* — it's about knowing the right things, avoiding common pitfalls, and mastering the moves that actually close deals.

This book won't hand you all the wisdom in the universe (let's keep it real), but it will arm you with battle-tested strategies, powerful frameworks, and insider tricks to make a difference where it matters. You'll find out how to navigate those sticky sales situations, sidestep potential deal-killers, and tackle every conversation with confidence.

It's the book that gives you just enough to stand out, take control, and win — without the fluff, but with a whole lot of punch.

About the Author

Since 1987, I've been on a journey through the fascinating world of sales, kicking off my career by selling floor and wall tiles, helping my customers transform their spaces into cozy retreats.

From those early days, I moved into more technical arenas — selling everything from amateur radio equipment to satellite image reception systems for weather satellites, all the way to high-stakes software solutions in fields like QA, cybersecurity, and complex automotive software, including ADAS, infotainment, and cockpit solutions.

My sales roles have taken me around the globe, from single-contributor positions to leading domain teams and selling across the US, EMEA, and APAC. Along the way, I've been responsible for quotas as modest as € 500 thousand to as large as €40 million. And while I've experienced my share of setbacks, I've also celebrated wins — some running into the multi-millions and even achieving a year's revenue of over €240 million with my team.

Through the ups and downs, the small wins and the big losses, one thing has stayed constant: my passion for the art and science of sales, and my commitment to sharing what I've learned along the way.

www.ingramcontent.com/pod-product-compliance
Lightning Source LLC
Chambersburg PA
CBHW071025240526
45469CB00006BD/2086